THE JOURNEY FROM FEELINGS TO FAITH

by

Carol Hopson

Published by:
Christian Services Network
833 Broadway, Suite #201
El Cajon, CA 92021
Toll Free: 1-866-484-6184
www.CSNbooks.com

Printed in the United States of America.

TABLE OF CONTENTS

iii

PREFACE

I looked longingly at my neighbor's bougainvillea bushes. They were full of bright red blooms in November and December and mine looked weak and forlorn, with no blooms in sight. Why such a difference? After six years of watching my plant bloom profusely for 4 months and then turn barren, I finally asked my husband to cut a large part of the tree down that shaded the plant for most of the winter. To my absolute delight, it is now flourishing, with full luscious blooms out my kitchen window...and it is January. What a difference the sun makes! It literally transformed this plant from empty, ugly branches, to the most beautiful sight.

I have enjoyed that climbing array of color so much these past months and it has often made me think about my own life. Oh, how I long to be healthy and full of beauty as a reflection of "the Son's" affect on my life. Sadly, there have been times when I've appeared barren because of not enough "Son exposure."

God declares:

My righteous one shall live by faith, and if he shrinks back, my soul has no pleasure in Him.
(Hebrews 10:38)

As I read this in my devotions, I was pierced in my heart because I knew that the Lord had found no pleasure in me at times. I thought I was living to please the Lord, but as the Holy Spirit convicted me, I realized that I had often lived by my feelings rather than by my faith, and so I write this book in obedience to God's call on my life to share what He has taught me about truly living by faith and staying in the Sonlight.

George Mueller, a great man of faith, once said,

Just in proportion to which we believe that God will do just what He has said, is our faith strong or weak. Faith has nothing to do with feelings, or with impressions, with improbabilities, or with outward appearances. Faith rests on the naked Word of God. When we take Him at His Word, the heart is at peace.

Let's begin the journey together.

CHAPTER 1

From Problems to Promises

What problems are you facing today? Do you feel overwhelmed and discouraged? Do you feel like there is no answer to your problem or that God isn't listening to you? Did you know that the man after God's own heart felt that way too? Listen to David's heart cry in Psalm 69:1-3:

> *Save me, O God, for the waters have threatened my life. I have sunk in deep mire, and there is no foothold; I have come into deep waters, and a flood overflows me. I am weary with my crying; my throat is parched; my eyes fail while I wait for my God.*

I too, have allowed my problems to become my focus and have felt such a heaviness that stayed with me like a dark cloud blotting out the sun in my life. I couldn't see any good that God was doing, only the pain of my situation and the hopeless feeling of not understanding what God was allowing. I've been betrayed by a close friend, hurt deeply by a relative, lied about in ministry, called to leave places I loved to obey God, suffered prolonged serious illnesses and so on...but through it all, I always had a choice to believe God's promise that *"All things work together for good to them that love God..."* (Romans 8:28a) or to focus on my problems and live by my negative feelings.

I was meeting with a woman recently who told me that she wakes up each morning and feels overwhelmed and depressed before she even gets out of bed because she thinks of all the problems and difficult circumstances in her life and she can hardly face the day. I asked her if she had ever played with one of those large magnets when she was a child. She said she had and I asked her what happened when the magnet was close to paper clips or pins? She responded that it drew them to it immediately and they clung to it. I then told her that our minds are like that magnet. God has given us the free will to focus on what we choose to, but so often, we attract the negatives in our lives because we spend our time thinking on them. You see, we can choose to be a magnet for good or evil thoughts in our minds. The choice is up to us! I've had to practice that over and over and over as I've had to leave unkind or untrue words in God's hands and focus on the truth of God's Word in every situation.

This past year, I had the great privilege of traveling to a foreign country to speak at a retreat for Arab world missionaries. I was humbled, grateful and excited about this ministry opportunity but as the trip grew closer, I began to feel overwhelmed and discouraged. I had been traveling for months already and was weary and didn't want to leave my dear husband again and travel so far away. I knew God had called me to do this, I knew it was the right thing to do, I knew God would see me through and yet…my mind kept focusing on the loneliness of the 10 days away, the difficulty of traveling so far, the unknown problems, my own weariness and all I'd be missing at home. You see, I had become a magnet for all the negatives involved in this trip and those thoughts spiraled me into discouragement.

I had only been home 5 days from a previous retreat and had to leave the next day for Amsterdam. I knew I had to get my heart in line with God's plan for me, so I sat in my family room and cried out to God. I told Him my deepest feelings and asked Him to replace those feelings with His joy and a renewed heart to serve Him. As I sat there quietly waiting on Him, He so lovingly brought to my mind that Jesus had left His home…not for 10 days or a few months, but for 33 years…for me! I was so overwhelmed with that thought that tears filled my eyes as I began to reflect on all Jesus went through on this earth for me and how he left all the comforts of "His home" just to save me, an unworthy child. My heart was so transformed as I felt God asking me, "Are you willing to leave for 10 more days so that others can be encouraged, renewed and refreshed by the words I've given you to share?" What a miraculous transformation took place in my heart that day! I left the next day eager, renewed and ready to serve my Savior who left all…just for me!

I'M LEAVING AGAIN

I'm leaving again and it's so hard
To catch another plane
And leave behind my husband dear
And head out for the rain.

I'm leaving all familiar things
For places yet unknown
For God has asked me yet again
To leave my comfort zone.

I find that Satan likes to use
These times away from home
To make me wish I didn't have
To leave and be alone.

But as I went to God in prayer
And asked Him for His strength
He told me in such loving words
"For you I went great lengths!"

"You see, my child, I left my home
because God knew your need
I stayed for thirty years and more
A very long time indeed.

But I did it for you because
I loved you from the start
Will you now leave your home for me
So others know my heart?

With new eyes now I see this trip
As something small to give
To Jesus who did leave His home
That I might forever live.

Carol Hopson

It's important to understand how those wrong, unhealthy thoughts take hold of our thinking, so let's look at some practical ways that we can "let go" and not be a magnet for the negative things in our lives.

In my experience, I have found that it is truly necessary to let go of my agenda and how I think my life should go. Proverbs 3:5-6 says to,

Trust in the Lord with all your heart and lean not on your own understanding. In all your ways acknowledge Him and He shall direct your path.

Notice that we are to trust in the Lord with ALL our heart, not just a part of it. That's totally trusting Him in all things whether we like the situation or not. It seems that I can so easily trust the Lord when God and I agree on what He is doing or allowing. I can even preach great messages on the subject. However, when God's plans and my idea of what is right and fair differ, I find myself so lacking in faith. This is when I must choose to trust with all my heart.

Secondly, we aren't to try to figure things out according to our understanding because it doesn't work. Again, to live by faith is to trust that God is working, especially when we don't see it or feel it and that becomes our true "love gift" to Him. Don't you love a gift that someone has sacrificed to give you? When my daughter has painted me a picture with her incredible talent, it is especially precious to me because of the sacrifice of time she made to do it with 3 small children to care for. When my dear husband takes me shopping and waits patiently while I look around or try things on, I am delighted by his sacrificial love because I know it's the last place on earth he would choose to be, except for his love for me. I see trusting God in the midst of our most difficult problems as that kind of love gift and it makes it all worthwhile.

Thirdly, we are to "acknowledge" or go to Him with all our grievances, misunderstandings, hurts and problems and listen to Him tell us what to do through His word, through prayer and through Godly counsel. Then we will see the path we are to take because we were listening to the right voice and not acting on our feelings.

We also need to let go of the past, whether good or bad. We need to let go of how things were in the past season of our lives and move on with an open heart, to what God has in store for us in the future. If our past season was one we loved but God is moving us into something new, we must trust Him enough to let go, to offer a sacrifice of thanksgiving for what He will do in this new season of our lives. Philippians 3:13 says we are to "forget what lies behind and reach forward to what lies ahead."

Maybe our past had relationships that we cherished and something has happened and we are hurting over the loss. Maybe we loved the work, the home, the ministry, the friendships, the place we lived etc. but God is allowing a change and we are struggling with it. Maybe, the past was full of failures and heartache and we have difficulty leaving it behind because we are so emotionally controlled by feelings of failure and negativity. No matter what our past situation, whether positive or negative, God says:

> *...it is God who is at work in you, both to will and to work for His good pleasure. Do all things without grumbling or disputing that you may prove*

yourselves to be blameless and innocent, children of God above reproach in a crooked and perverse generation, among whom you appear as lights in the world.

(Philippians 2:13-15)

God promises to help us in this new season, He will do the work in us if we allow Him to so that we will shine as lights in this world as we accept changes without grumbling or complaining, but with a trusting heart. Remember that God promises,

He who began a good work in you, will continue to perform it until the day of Jesus Christ.

(Philippians 1:6)

Whatever God is allowing in your life will be used to bring about His good work in you until He returns. God's sovereignty and love aren't measured by the problems He helps us avoid or the pleasant circumstances He allows us to enjoy, but by His ability to accomplish His purpose through every circumstance. (Romans 8:28)

Lloyd John Ogilvie wrote,

Where do you need a miracle, what to you seems impossible? Persist! Don't give up! At all costs make your way to the Master. Tell Him your need and then leave it with Him. Even greater than the miracle you seek will be the miracle you become by seeking Him, touching Him and experiencing His matchless love.

Will you be a magnet for problems or God's promises today? It's your choice!

Personal check-up:

If living in light of your problems...

You'll often think on things that make you bitter or negative.

You'll associate with or listen to others who bring you down or agree with your negative outlook.

You won't spent much time in prayer or in God's Word.

Life will seem overwhelming and unbearable at times.

You'll begin to doubt God's love and His promises.

If living in light of God's promises...

You'll begin and end the day with God's Word in your heart.

You will memorize a verse that will comfort you throughout the day.

You will associate with those who lift you up and encourage you spiritually.

You'll replace negative thoughts with thankful, positive thoughts.

You'll know God's peace as you leave your problems in His hands.

Bible Study Questions for Chapter 1 are on page 125.

CHAPTER 2

From Grit to Grace

Have you been through times recently, when you've just tried to "grit your teeth" and somehow get through your situation? Your jaw is tight, your stomach churns, you're angry with yourself and others, but you will toughen up and somehow get through life's trials. Did you know that God offers a much better way to live, and that is by grace. To live by grace is to realize that you can't handle life's problems on your own, and you need your Maker's help; you need Him to enable you to do what you could not do in your own strength. Paul recognized this when He wrote:

I can do all things through Him who strengthens me.

(Philippians 4:13)

A woman came to me for counsel who was truly living by grit. She was angry, tough and even looked like she was gritting her teeth as she spoke of all the unfair situations in her life. She began telling me of her husband's emotional beatings that she had endured for over 20 years and then how he added physical abuse in the latter years. She went on to share that her teenage children would join in and batter her with words also, following their father's example. After years and years of this terrible abuse, her children left home, her husband finally left her and she became a recluse in her own home. She couldn't leave it for over 10 years and became a virtual prisoner of her own fears, failures and low self-esteem.

One day, a frequent visitor brought her a book I had written. She loved to read and eagerly read it and later told the woman that she wished she could meet the author. The friend picked up on this and told her I would be speaking at their church retreat in a few months and maybe she'd like to attend it so she could meet me. The woman stared at her in unbelief and yet had a small, hopeful feeling that maybe she could try. For the next few months, this friend worked with her to help her open her front door and stand there...it was terrifying to her. Then she would try to take one step out the door and would run back in...more terrified. Eventually, after many tears and painful first steps, she was able to leave her house and eventually came to the retreat to meet me.

16

When I met her I was overwhelmed with all she'd been through in her life and all she'd accomplished to get to the retreat. I also was aware of the anger and "grit" that she lived with and felt so sorry for her. There was no joy, no peace and no purpose in her life, only anger, which was understandable from a human perspective. I had to admit to her that I could never understand the pain she had suffered and wouldn't even try. But I knew someone who did understand...Jesus. The more we talked, the more she began to soften her jaw, open her a heart a little and listen. The Holy Spirit was working and she eventually gave her life to the Lord. Here's where the "grit or grace" comes in. She now had the power within her to live by grace and give up the anger she had held for so long.

God brought the following verses to mind to share with her:

Be still in the presence of the Lord, and wait patiently for Him to act. Don't worry about evil people who prosper or fret about their wicked schemes. Stop your anger, turn from your rage! Do not envy others, it only leads to harm. For the wicked will be destroyed but those who trust in the Lord will possess the land.

(Psalm 37:7-9, NLT)

You shall know the truth and the truth shall make you free.

(John 8:32)

I came that you might have life, and might have it abundantly.

(John 10:10)

The only way to abundant, joyful living is to leave all of the anger and unfair situations in the hands of the Righteous Judge. We need to realize that bitterness and anger only hurt us and keep us from moving on into the productive, power-filled life God has promised those who trust in Him. I told her that hanging on to bitterness was like eating rat poison and then waiting for the rat to die!

As she wept and gave up all her years of anger, fear and resentment to the Lord, I observed the huge weight being lifted from her. She actually smiled when she finished praying...it was a beautiful smile! There would still be doubts and difficult moments to face, but now she knew that "God's grace was sufficient" to meet her needs and she knew that carrying that huge weight of bitterness was only harming her. She now had a new focus in life and was eager to live in this newly found freedom.

Do you find yourself living by "grit" rather than by "grace"? I've been guilty many times and have had to confess this over and over, but the great news is that Jesus forgives me every time. (1 John 1:9) The more I learn to live by grace, the more free I am to love and serve my Savior. To live my life by grace is to make the following choices in my life each day:

To make it easier to remember, I'll use the word "life" to illustrate each point.

L – Let go of wrong thinking and expectations

I – Influence others for Christ daily

F – Forgive others quickly

E – Express praise continually

18

Let's look at each one of these in light of what God desires of us.

L – Let go of wrong thinking and expectations.

We need to let go of wrong thinking and expectations. I need to be reminded of this so often. We expect people to change...our mates, our children, our friends, our co-workers...and then are upset when they don't. I remember that I expected a certain relative to change every time I saw him and when he didn't, I'd be so disappointed and discouraged. I'd try harder to be acceptable, to be perfect, to be what he thought I should be and yet, I'd get the same negative reaction. It wasn't until I gave it all to the Lord and realized that my only hope was in God's love and acceptance of me that I found peace. I needed to give up my unreal expectations of this person and find my joy and self-worth in the Lord. It changed everything, especially me!

We also expect circumstances to change quickly or to go as we hoped they would. We expect to not be hurt or disappointed by people. You see, we put our hope in people or circumstances and then are frustrated or angry when they don't measure up to our expectations. This can destroy marriages and family relationships because it causes unreal pressure on others and our hope is in the wrong place, it belongs only in God. Hebrews 6:19 tells us that:

...this hope we have as an anchor for our souls, a hope both sure and steadfast...

To be emotionally anchored, we need to let go of our expectations of people, and put all our hope in our unchanging, faithful God. David said:

My soul, wait in silence for God only, for my hope is from Him.

(Psalm 62:5)

I – Influence others for Christ daily.

You might wonder how this is a part of living by grace but it comes from 1 Peter 4:10,

As each one has received a special gift employ it in serving one another, as good stewards of the manifold grace of God.

And 2 Corinthians 2:14-16 reminds us that,

...Christ manifests through us, the sweet aroma of the knowledge of Him in every place. For we are a fragrance of Christ to God among those who are being saved and among those who are perishing.

Living by grace involves giving others the grace we have received. It involves being a sweet aroma, someone who draws others to Christ by the way we act, speak and live our daily lives. The other day, my husband was away on a business trip and I was up very early on a Sunday morning so decided to take my Bible and notebook and head to Starbucks before church. It has become my habit to pray as I leave the house, and ask God to use me to share His love with someone who needs it. I pray that He will make me aware of others around me who may be hurting or lonely and then I prayerfully yield myself to Him for however He chooses to use me. When I arrived at Starbucks, it was so early that no one else was there except me and those behind the counter. After buying my drink, I sat down at one of the many empty tables and began studying my Bible and taking notes. Shortly, a very thin, poorly dressed woman came in and I smiled at her as she walked by and she went to buy her drink. When she came back, she looked at the 5 empty tables along one wall and looked at the one table on the opposite side where I was sitting. Again, I smiled at her, said good morning, and continued with my study. She proceeded to my small table and took the chair on the opposite side, turned her back to me and sat down facing the wall...at my table! Now I could have two different reactions, one would be to wonder why she was invading my space when my table was full, I was obviously busy and all the other tables were empty. The other reaction would be that this was a divine appointment and I was meant to give grace to her and be that sweet aroma that draws others to Christ. Only by God's grace, I chose the latter. As she sat with her back to me, I said, "Good morning". There was no response and so I tried it again. Again, there was no response, just her back sitting there at my table only 3 feet away. What a strange situation this was. I went back to my Bible reading and began to pray, "Lord this is so unusual and I know You must have led me here early this morning to share Your love with this woman, but what do I do?" I knew I should just wait. After about 10 minutes, which seemed like a very long time, she turned around and pointed to my pen. I asked her if she wanted it and she shook her head that she did. I handed it to her and she got up and got several napkins from the stand and began writing. The first thing she wrote was, "Do you go to church?" I asked if she could read lips and she said she could so I proceeded to tell her "Yes, I go to church and I am a Christian. I feel God has sent me here this morning to tell you that He loves you." The tears began to flow as she wrote me of her disease and how she couldn't speak or hear. We wrote back and forth for about half an hour and I was able to pray with her, share God's love with her and then I hugged her as she got up to leave. She seemed so overwhelmed with a loving touch.

I don't know what happened in her life after that, but I do know that influencing others for Christ is what we are called to do and it gives us more joy than anything on this earth. I did go to Starbucks for the next 3 Sunday mornings to see if she would be there again but I haven't seen her since. However, God sees her and she now knows of His great love for her.

F – Forgive others quickly.

This is one of the most important ways we can pass on God's grace to others, by forgiving them. Ephesians 4:31 and 32 counsels us to,

> *Get rid of all bitterness, rage, anger, harsh words and slander, as well as all types of malicious behavior. Instead, be kind to each other, tender-hearted, forgiving one another, just as God through Christ has forgiven you.*
>
> (Ephesians 4:31-32, NLT)

Did you notice that God doesn't say to forgive others because they deserve it? That always helps me to realize that He understands that some people are really hard to forgive because we honestly feel that they don't deserve forgiveness. By forgiving, we are not saying that the person was right in his or actions because many times that is not the case. But again, God tells us that the reason we are to forgive is because Christ forgave us. We are to pass on the grace, the undeserved favor of God, to those who hurt us, out of love and gratitude to our Savior.

This does not mean that we become a doormat for abuse, or say that the abuse or unjust treatment should be overlooked; but it does mean that we are willing to forgive when someone asks for our forgiveness and it also means that we give the hurt to the Lord. We give up our anger and bitterness towards that person out of our love for the Lord and in obedience to His command. Remember God's clear direction for is in 1 Peter 2:21-23,

For you have been called for this purpose, since Christ also suffered for you, leaving you an example for you to follow in His steps, who committed no sin, nor was any deceit found in His mouth; and while being reviled, He did not revile in return; while suffering, He uttered no threats, but kept entrusting Himself to Him who judges righteously.

God's plan is that we follow Christ's example in how we act and react and then we leave the judgment of that person's deeds to Almighty God who will be the Righteous Judge. What freedom there is in forgiveness!

MUST I FORGIVE?

Here I am again dear Lord
Needing to forgive
But I'm not really sure if that's
The way I want to live.

You see it's not so easy
For me to just let go
Of all the things I see and hear
And words that hurt me so.

23

I want to be like you, dear Lord
In all I do and say.
But does that mean I must forgive?
Is there some other way?

And then I heard His answer
As clearly as can be,
"When you forgive, dear child of mine,
is when you're most like me!"

Carol Hopson

E – Express praise continually.

While going through a very difficult time recently, I came upon Hebrews 13:15 and found that it was the answer to my emotional and spiritual needs and it brought me back to living by grace in some very trying circumstances. It says,

Through Him then, let us continually offer up a sacrifice of thanksgiving, that is the fruit of lips that give praise to His name.

As the Holy Spirit worked in my heart, He showed me the four aspects of this verse that were life-transforming and I have continued to use this verse for encouragement and direction many, many times. Here are the four things we need to know:

"Through Him then"

It is by Jesus' power alone that I can handle a difficult situation gracefully. It is by Jesus' power in me that I can hug a person who has deeply offended or hurt me or someone I love. It is by His power and presence in my life that

I can forgive and by His power I can find reasons to praise Him in any situation.

And He has said to me, 'My grace is sufficient for you for power is perfected in weakness.' Most gladly, therefore, I will rather boast about my weaknesses, that the power of Christ may dwell in me...for when I am weak, then I am strong.
(2 Corinthians 12:9-10b)

I find that when I'm feeling down or discouraged or even a little angry, it's because I'm saying "no thanks to the Holy Spirit's power in my life, and I'm saying "yes" to self! How that must grieve my Lord.

"Let us continually"

In this passage, we are told that our praise should be continual, not just when something good has happened or when we understand what God is doing. It should constantly flow from our hearts as David said in Psalm 34:1:

I will bless the Lord at all times: His praise shall continually be in my mouth.

Do you know why praise is so important in the believer's life?

- You can't be bitter and praise God at the same time.
- Praise defeats Satan.
- Praise is an act of obedience to God.
- Praise turns your thoughts from your problems to God's power.
- Praise keeps your heart in fellowship with the Lord.

Let me give you a beautiful example of what it means to praise God continually. I was called to come to a dear friend's home because her son had died very suddenly that morning. I went there to comfort her, hold her and pray with her, but as the morning passed and many came to show their love and sympathy, I noticed something remarkable. I kept hearing this precious mother say things like, "I'm so thankful for my friends and family. I'm so thankful that my other sons were here. I'm so thankful for God's grace. I'm so thankful for all the prayers for me and my family. I'm so thankful that God has a reason for this even though it hurts so much." Throughout the days that led up to the Memorial Service, I continually heard her give thanks to the Lord for one thing or another. She was not thanking God for taking her son, but she was thanking Him for His provision and special grace in the midst of all she and her husband were experiencing. What a testimony!

When you're having a rough day, do you find yourself continually praising God? It's a tough question, isn't it? But the more I practice this, the more I see how God uses praise to heal my spirit, keep my focus clear and bless those around me. Remember God's words, *"...Praise is becoming to the upright."* Ps. 33:1b

"Offer up a sacrifice of thanksgiving"

It is so clear to me that being thankful often requires a sacrifice. What am I sacrificing...my plan and my will! You see to sacrifice something is to give up something we highly value for something or someone we value more highly. Therefore, when I continually praise God in any situation, I am "giving up" my will and accepting God's will and praising Him for what He will do in me, for me and through me. Let's just look at an everyday, simple illus-

26

tration of what I think God wants in us. Over Christmas, I got a very bad cold and cough and felt fairly horrible. Yet, I was going to be with family and had lots of responsibilities and didn't want to ruin it for everyone else. During the night, when needing my rest, I would cough uncontrollably and be unable to get to sleep. Now, am I still supposed to praise God continually...when I feel lousy...when I can't stop coughing...when I'm not getting any rest? Well, I don't see any "exception clauses" in God's word, do you? I've been looking a long time and I have yet to find a verse that says, "be thankful except when you're really sick or miserable". And, I haven't found a verse that says, "Trust God most of time, unless something really horrible happens and you can't understand it." It's just not there! So, to be a follower of Christ, I must take God's Word and follow it implicitly.

Now, how would you praise God with that horrible cold? Here's what God showed me. I began thanking Him for my warm home, my comfortable bed, that I could get up and have a cup of tea in the night, that I had a loving family who cared about me, that this would someday pass and I would feel better, that He was with me and knew how I felt...and so on. I still had the cold, but my spirit was better because I was praising God for what I could and leaving the results with Him. I believe that when it's most difficult to be thankful, it brings the most joy to our Savior.

He who offers a sacrifice of thanksgiving honors Me...

(Psalm 50:23)

"The fruit of lips that give praise to His Name"

This portion of the verse tells me that not only should I have an inward attitude of praise, but it should flow outwardly, "from my lips" to those around me. Others should be blessed by my attitude of thanksgiving! Wow...do you think that is the way you are touching others for Christ? Remember the mother who just lost her son? Would I, or others, have been so blessed and encouraged if she had kept all of her praise to herself? It was in her outward expression of praise that I was so touched and encouraged by how God's grace had met her needs and brought her peace. I truly want to be one who blesses others by the way I outwardly praise God in any situation.

Will you determine before God, to make these four life choices each day? Put them in your Bible, on your nightstand or refrigerator as a reminder. I have mine posted by my desk as a constant checklist as to what choices I'm making each day. If you choose to live by them, God will turn your life around and help you give up the "grit" and live by His amazing "grace".

PERSONAL CHECKUP:

If living by grit:

You'll be easily angered over something you hear.

You'll rehearse the negatives in your life.

You'll strike out at others because of your unresolved anger.

You'll condemn others for things you are guilty of.

You'll be tense and irritable and unable to find peace.

If living by grace:

You'll remember God's grace to you, with a thankful heart.

You'll desire to pass on that grace to others.

You will seek to forgive others quickly, with God's help.

You will desire to please God by the way you live.

You will be excited about influencing others for Christ.

Bible Study Questions for Chapter 2 are on page 129.

CHAPTER 3

From Regretting to Rejoicing

We all have regrets, don't we? Some have more than others but we all have them. We can get so lost in our feelings of regret that we lose the joys of today and the hopes for tomorrow. Let me tell you of a place where there were more regrets than I had ever seen.

I had been asked to speak in a women's prison and give a Christmas message. In this prison, the women were only allowed to get together like this once a year and this was their big event. How and why I was asked to speak is something only God knows. I readily accepted the invitation and then began to ask myself, "What will I say? What do I have in common with those women? How can they relate to me? I've never done drugs, been arrested, been in prison...and I have a lovely home and a loving husband and family. How can I possibly relate to their situation and why would they listen to me?" As I pondered this and began praying about it, the Lord seemed to penetrate my heart with this prayer. "Lord, remove Carol and let them see only Jesus." I prayed it over and over and over for the four months leading up to the event. Every time it would come to my mind I'd repeat, "Let them see Jesus, only Jesus!"

The time was drawing closer and I now needed to prepare my message. I had been asked to speak for about an hour and I kept asking God to give me His wisdom as to what I should share. I had many Christmas messages in my file and new ones I had just written for Christmas Teas and Banquets this year, but none of them seemed quite right for women in prison. I kept praying. I finally wrote the message I thought God wanted me to give and left it in His hands. When the Sunday night came, my husband drove me to a drop-off place where I was picked up and taken about thirty miles farther to the prison. It was a dark, cold, rainy night and I had no idea where we were as we headed way up in the mountains. Upon our arrival, I had to be frisked and checked out. I had been given very little information as to what was expected of me, what I could or couldn't say or do and so I just walked on in faith.

A guard took me to the cafeteria, which was the only room big enough to hold the meeting. As I sat up at the front, I kept pleading with God that they would see Jesus' love for them and that I, Carol, wouldn't be a stumbling block. I watched as each inmate walked in the back door and stared up at me. I smiled broadly and tried to make eye contact with each one, while saying inwardly, "Let them see Jesus!" I could see so much in their faces...anger, bitterness, hurt, low self-esteem, regret. How was I going to meet those needs in one message? You can't imagine how inadequate I felt, but God had given me His promise that "our adequacy is not of ourselves, but of God" and so I was truly at peace.

After a few Christmas Carols, I was introduced. Here's the situation: I had my notes in a folder and my Bible and now I was handed a microphone with no stand. I suddenly noticed that there was no table, no podium and no place to put my Bible and notes while I held the microphone. I knew I couldn't be fumbling with notes and my Bible and keep eye contact with all those women. The Holy Spirit spoke to me in His quiet voice at that moment and said, "Leave your notes and Bible back on the seat and I'll give you the message I want you to share with these women. Trust Me!" And so that's what I did. I put everything down behind me except the microphone and I looked out at the sea of orange jumpsuits and said, "My grandson, Jack, would just love to be standing here right now!" That got their attention. "Do you know what his favorite color is?" I asked. And they shouted back at me "Orange?" "You got it!" I replied. They clapped and cheered and it seemed that the ice had been broken and now I was truly relying on the Holy Spirit to do His work.

> *For it is God Who is at work in you, both to will and to do His good pleasure.*
>
> (Philippians 2:13)

I began by admitting to them that I had no idea what their life was like. I had never been in prison and couldn't know their hurts, their pain, their anger and their regrets. I told them that I didn't know what life was like for them inside those walls. At that precise moment, God gave me the new message He had for them and so I said, "But I do know about the prisons on the outside of these walls." It seemed like every eye turned to look and every ear was ready to listen at that point. I had been warned that they might turn their backs on me, or act up in some way or just ignore me, but so far, they were listening. God then brought to my mind, three women whom I had recently counseled who were imprisoned by fear or resentment or guilt and I began to tell their stories. Because I had no notes, I was free to walk close to them and make eye contact with them while the Holy Spirit was speaking through me. I told them how God had broken down the prison walls for each woman and how they had found such freedom and joy when they met Jesus. I explained how God loved them so much that He sent His only Son, Jesus, to die for all the wrong they had ever done or would ever do. I went on to share how these women's lives were transformed because of the freedom from guilt and the forgiveness of sins they experienced, I really don't know exactly what I said because the Holy Spirit had taken over and the unplanned message just kept flowing. After forty-five minutes, I explained that Christmas was about this incredible gift of "freedom" and "new beginnings" through God's Son, Jesus. And, I told them that He had sent me there to tell them how much He loved them and cared about them. They were told that even though they would still be behind those prison walls, they could feel totally free in their hearts and have a new reason for living.

When I had finished, I asked them to close their eyes while I prayed. Then I asked if anyone wanted to "break out" from the prison of self-condemnation, guilt, resentment, bitterness etc., and if they did, I asked them to repeat the prayer of repentance and acceptance after me. I didn't know if this was allowed but felt it would be easier to ask forgiveness later than to ask for permission now. As I prayed, my heart was pleading with God to let the women see the love of Jesus in me and let someone respond to His message of hope. After praying the prayer of salvation, I asked them to keep their eyes closed and raise their hand if anyone had prayed that prayer with me. To my utter shock, over fifty hands went up and I began to hear weeping. Thinking that they had misunderstood the question, I told them to put their hands down and again explained what it meant to ask God for forgiveness and what it meant to belong to Him and turn from their sinful ways. Then, I asked for the raised hands again and over fifty women raised their hands again. Through my tears I prayed again and thanked God for this miracle.

This precious treasure, this light and power that now shine within us, is held in perishable containers, that is, in our weak bodies. So everyone can see that our glorious power is from God and is not our own.

(2 Corinthians 4:7, NLT)

I then had to go back to my little stool at the front of the cafeteria and sit and wait for them to be served dessert, the main attraction of the night. While sitting there and looking out at all those tear-stained faces, I felt such a tug on my heart and thought, "What would Jesus do now?" It came so quickly that I didn't have time to think about it. He would touch them! So, I got up and went to the first table and said, "Would anyone here like a hug from Jesus?" The first woman popped up and threw her arms around me and started weeping. The first words she spoke in my ear were "I was supposed to get out of here last week, but it got postponed and I'm so glad because I wouldn't have met Jesus today! It was like He was here speaking to us." Do you remember my daily prayer leading up to this event? It was, "Lord, let them see Jesus, not Carol."

After that, every person at that table stood up to be hugged and then I went to the next table and the next and every single person in that prison waited to be hugged. They whispered all sorts of things in my ears, mostly thank you for bringing Jesus to the prison and many shared that they had prayed the prayer and that they had never felt so loved before. Some were just silent, but no one rejected the hug. It took almost a half hour to get to every table. Here's another part of the miracle. The guards stood along the walls and did absolutely nothing to stop me. It was only when I was being escorted back to the car that I was told that no one was ever allowed to touch the inmates because they could take you hostage or injure you or something. I politely smiled and said, "I guess God didn't know that!"

If those women could give up their regrets and turn to rejoicing, can't we do the same? We put ourselves in such prisons over what happened yesterday, last week, last year or ten years ago.

God says,

> Don't worry about anything; instead, pray about
> everything. Tell God what you need and thank him
> for all he has done. If you do this, you will experi-
> ence God's peace, which is far more wonderful than
> the human mind can understand. His peace will
> guard your hearts and minds as you live in Christ
> Jesus.
>
> (Philippians 4:6-7, NLT)

To accept God's peace, we need to ask forgiveness for
our sins and wrong choices and then leave them all at the
cross. Jesus paid the debt for all of it already and if we try
to carry the burden of guilt or anger, we are saying to Him
that His death didn't matter and He didn't do enough to
free us. I just don't ever want to do that and so I choose to
leave my regrets behind and rejoice in today and tomorrow
and all God can and will do as I choose to live for Him.

I vividly remember one retreat at which I was speaking. For the last message, we had put a huge, rough-hewn
cross on the stage. After the message, I asked that each
person would write their biggest regret or sin on the 3x5
card they had been given. During the prayer time, I asked
each one who wanted to be truly free, to come forward and
hammer that card to the cross, face down. Almost everyone came forward and tearfully hammered their regrets to
the cross. When they had all finished, I took a huge sign
and nailed it on the cross that said, "Paid in full!" Then we
sang together, "Jesus paid it all, all to Him I owe. Sin had
left a crimson stain, He washed me white as snow."

37

You were dead because of your sins and because your sinful nature was not yet cut away. Then God made you alive with Christ, He forgave all our sins. He cancelled the record that contained the charges against us. He took it and destroyed it by nailing it to Christ's cross.

(Colossians 2:13-14, NLT)

Isn't it time to turn your regretting into rejoicing?

Personal Check-up

If focusing on your regrets:

You'll have a heaviness in your heart each day.

You'll continually rehearse the hurtful situation or poor choices.

You will choose to neglect God's forgiveness and grace.

You'll miss the opportunities and joys God has for you each day.

If choosing to rejoice:

You'll be sad over your past but will leave it ALL at the cross.

You'll readily ask forgiveness when Satan brings your mind back to your failures or hurts.

You'll choose to thank God daily for all He has done and continues to do in your life.

Bible Study Questions for Chapter 3 are on page 133.

CHAPTER 4

From Selfishness to Godliness

Well, this chapter title really sums up what we want in life. It gets down to the very core of our thinking. I was talking to a woman last week who summed up her thoughts like this. "I just want to be happy and have my children be happy. Is that too much to ask?" She said she had accepted the Lord early in her life and had been serving in the church for many years. She and her family went to church regularly, she attended weekly Bible study and her children were in a Christian school. It sounds like she would have a corner on Godliness, doesn't it? Sadly, those are not the ingredients of Godliness.

What this woman was missing was a clear under-standing of the purpose of the Christian life. God did not send His Son to earth to make us "happy"; He sent His Son to make us "Holy" or Christ-like. Look at Peter's words in 1 Peter 1:13-16,

> *Therefore, gird your minds for action, keep sober in spirit, fix your hope completely on the grace to be brought to you at the revelation of Jesus Christ. As obedient children, do not be conformed to your for-mer lusts, which were yours in your ignorance, but like the Holy One Who called you, be holy your-selves also in all your behavior: because it is writ-ten, 'You shall be holy, for I am holy.'*

As I've watched my own children grow up, and now my five precious grandchildren, I've seen a common pattern in their young lives. They think about what will make them happy and they want it no matter what. They don't under-stand waiting or money issues or what would be best for them. This is because of their immaturity and self-cen-teredness. This is normal for a young child who has not yet learned the importance of thinking of others first or living for the Lord. They need to be taught by word and example how to live in a way that pleases God. We expect this in children, it is the way they are made. But when we see it in a full grown adult, it's more difficult to understand.

God promises peace, forgiveness, freedom from guilt, joy, purpose, contentment and much more in His word. But, He never promises a "happy life" and I think many Christians think that this is what a Christian life is about. Why then would we desire Godliness? I've been asked that question dozens of times after I've shared a message on

42

giving up your rights and your will and going with God's plan. Let me answer it this way. Do you know someone who has finally found her "niche" and just loves what she does? I have a friend who was never content, never satisfied and always a little edgy...until she discovered gardening and growing things, drying things, arranging flower etc. She eventually turned it into a business and told me over and over that this is what she was created to do. She was truly a different person once she discovered what fulfilled her. This is different from spiritual fulfillment but it does illustrate why we should desire Godliness. You see, God created each of us to reflect His love and live a Godly life for the world to see. When we aren't fulfilling that purpose, there is a vacuum in our hearts and emotions that only God can fill.

Though my life has not been easy and God has taken me through some very deep valleys, I wouldn't trade my journey for anything this world offers. The reason is that I have peace and the deepest joy, not happiness, but inward joy that comes from doing what I was created to do...to know, love and serve my Savior. Nothing that this world offers compares to it.

Do not love the world, nor the things in the world. If anyone loves the world, the love of the Father is not in him. For all that is in the world, the lust of the flesh and the lust of the eyes and the boastful pride of life, is not from the Father, but is from the world. And the world is passing away and also its lusts; but the one who does the will of God abides forever.

(1 John 2:15-17)

Before we talk more about Godliness, it is essential to understand that we must have a relationship with the Savior in order to live Godly lives. Let's look at it this way, before I fell in love with my husband, before I knew all the qualities that I admired in him, before I knew of his deep love for me, I couldn't think of being married to him. The development of the love relationship preceded the commitment and devotion, and it's the same way in our Christian life. Having a heart to truly love God and get to know Him more and more is the only way we can live a Godly life.

In order to develop a close, loving relationship with someone, we need to spend time together, getting to know how the other person thinks and what is important to him or her. We share our joys, our sorrows, our failures, our dreams. We listen, we laugh, we cry and we love just being together. In the same way, we need to share every area of our lives with Almighty God and study His word to know what he is thinking, what is important to Him and how to live in a way that pleases Him.

Once we've made a commitment of our lives to God, we will then move from selfishness to Godliness. Here are some of the ways Godliness is exhibited in a believer's life.

Since this book is about living by faith, not feelings, I think we should discuss faith first. A simple definition for faith is "taking God at His word and acting accordingly". To illustrate this, let me tell you about my 91-year-old mother.

Two years ago, my mother had a routine colonoscopy and we thought she was fine but I got a call that she was in intensive care and was not expected to live through the night due to a puncture in the colon. She was 89 years old at the time. I caught a flight from California to Idaho in the next couple of hours and thought I probably wouldn't make it in time but was trusting God for whatever He had in store. My mother did make it through the night and through the next 10 days in intensive care. I sat by her bedside along with my dad and other relatives, praying for God's will and releasing her to God's plan for her life. It was a miracle that she lived but we were told that she wouldn't walk again and would probably remain in a nursing home. Well, God had other plans and my mother did learn to walk again and after months of therapy, she was able to return home and live with my dad. She was able to drive again, she went shopping, out to eat, to church and she and my dad even drove all the way to San Diego to visit me. Amazing! Well, six months later, my dear mother tripped while walking into church and broke her pelvis and her arm in four places. She was now 90 years old and again, the doctors said, she will not be able to recover and learn to walk again. But, again, God had a different plan and my mother worked so hard in her therapy, both in learning to walk and in using her arm and wrist, that she did learn to walk again, even without a walker. We were all rejoicing and praising God and calling my mother "the energizer bunny" because she just kept going and going. It was painful and so difficult for someone that age to go through again, but she kept trusting the Lord and trying hard to do all she could to get well.

She just received a clean bill of health from the doctor last June and she and my Dad were so excited and grateful. Then, on July 4th, she had a major stroke and collapsed in her closet while getting ready to go to a party. I wondered how much my dear mother and dad could take as my husband and I flew up there again. When I saw my mother in intensive care again, I knew in my heart that she couldn't come back from such a major stroke, and all the doctors agreed and prepared us that she would not be leaving the hospital. It was several days after the stroke that my mother was trying to talk to me and I was asking her how she was feeling. In that very slow, painstaking, stroke victim voice she said to me, "If this is what God wants, I'll do my best to accept it and get well again." I wept! That is the best example of faith I can share with you. She was taking God at His word and acting accordingly...no matter what!

Do you want to hear the rest of the story? My mother baffled the doctors again. She was in the hospital and nursing home for several months of extensive therapy and then was released to move home with my dad again. And yes, she did learn to walk again, (the third time in two years), to speak very well, to feed herself and she even writes an occasional letter to me again! What a testimony she has been of never giving up or living by your feelings, but by your faith in what God can do.

Another way we exhibit Godliness is found in Colossians 3:12-17 where we read that we are to "put on" or be clothed with "*a heart of compassion, kindness, humility, gentleness and patience; bearing with one another and forgiving each other...*" The "bearing with" one another is forbearance, which means that we are to accept others as they are, not as we wish they were. Oh dear, does that bring conviction to your heart like it does to mine? Yes, Godliness involves accepting others the way God made them and loving them, praying for them and thinking the best of them. Philippians 2:3 reminds us that we are to *"do nothing from selfishness or conceit, but with humility of mind, let each of you regard one another as more important than himself."* Isn't that the way God sees us? He accepts us as we are, loves us and patiently leads us toward maturity. How can we show this type of love or forbearance to a child, family member, friend or co-worker?

- By not expecting them to live up to our dreams.

- By helping them move towards Godly living but not expecting them to have arrived.

- By looking for the good things God has created in them.

- By not comparing them to others who seem more loving or more spiritually mature.

- By praying daily for them and thanking God for them.

- By being a loving example of God's grace and forgiveness.

Another quality we are to be clothed with is humility. When you think of all Jesus went through for us, do you think of a proud, haughty spirit or a humble spirit, willing to suffer, to endure the hatred of men, to be misunderstood and rejected? He truly was the perfect example of humility. We read in Philippians 2:5-8 that He willingly gave up His rights, emptied self and humbly obeyed His heavenly Father. But humility is not a very popular word these days. Everywhere I look, I hear people saying that we should "stand up for our rights" and "we deserve the best' and "I'll do it my way". Sadly, none of these are part of Godly living.

We read in 1 peter 5:6,

Humble yourselves therefore under the mighty hand of God, that he may exalt you at the proper time, casting all your anxiety upon Him, because He cares for you.

Matthew Henry's commentary puts it this way, "Let your minds, behavior, garb and whole frame be adorned with humility, as the most beautiful habit you can wear; this will render obedience and duty easy and pleasant." If we are to be "adorned" or clothed with humility, we need to know what it is. The word humble means a lack of pride, aware of one's own shortcomings, modest, showing differential respect to others. So, here are some ways that we put on the Godly clothing of humility so that our lives will reflect Christ.

We would be aware of our own faults and not so quick to judge others.

Philippians 2:3-4

We wouldn't dwell on hurt feelings, but on God's love and healing power.

Ephesians 4:31-32

We would accept the place, situation and circumstances God has allowed, and seek to use them for His glory.

We wouldn't worry about what people think of us, but would be concerned only about what God thinks.

Colossians 1:10

We would allow God to work in us and through us, however He chooses.

Romans 8:28

We wouldn't get angry at people or unjust situations but would leave the results and judgment with Him.

1 Peter 2:21-13

We would not seek praise on this earth, but would wait for God to exalt us.

James 4:10

How is your "humility wardrobe"? Has it been sitting in your closet a while? Have you been seeking the praise of men or the praise of God? As we reflect on the theme of this chapter, living by selfishness or Godliness, we see that it all comes down to the decisions we make in each situation. Either we will try to exalt self, with prideful reactions, or we will wait for God to exalt us, by exemplifying Godly humility.

God is opposed to the proud, but gives grace to the humble.
Humble yourselves in the presence of the Lord, and He will exalt you.

(James 4:6 and 10)

There are many more aspects of Godliness but I just wanted to begin to make you aware of what will be evident in our lives as we grow closer to the Savior and learn to love Him more. But always remember that it is the Holy Spirit who does the work in us as we submit ourselves and our wills to God.

As we finish up this chapter, I'd like to share with you why we go back to selfishness so quickly, and how we can have more victory in this area. I was recently speaking at a retreat where a new song was being introduced, and this line stood out to me; "I can never return, I've closed the door. I will walk the path, I'll run the race, and I will never be the same again." As I listened to the words, God spoke so directly to my heart. I was getting ready to get up and share a whole weekend of messages. I was the one teaching and inspiring others, but here I was, convicted of how often I had not closed the door...on selfish desires...on bitter thoughts...on worry. As I sat there, God showed me a picture of a doorframe with a closed door, sitting up on the stage. I pictured my worries, and anxious or disgruntled thoughts on one side of the door, On the other side of the door was peace, forgiveness and freedom. One side was self-centered, the other was God-centered. The only way to get from one side to the other was to open the door and walk through.

I realized that opening that door and walking through was the process of praying, asking God for forgiveness, giving up my pride and leaving all my struggles and unresolved problems with Him. As I walked through that door, there was complete freedom and peace as I moved on *to walk in a manner worthy of the Lord, to please Him in all respects...*" Colossians 1:10a. The key was to "close the door" and never return! It was then that the Holy Spirit again convicted me of how often I have gone back, after being delivered into God's amazing freedom, and have willingly opened the door to discouraging or negative thoughts. It is like saying, "Come in Satan, you are welcome to destroy my peace and joy." You see, He has no power when I'm rightly walking with the Lord, his power is only in the past, the sin, the fears that I pick up and carry again. It was truly overwhelming to realize that I make the choice to open that door to self-centered thoughts that destroy my peace. It is also overwhelming to realize that, by God's power and grace, I can close the door, walk the righteous path and never return.

It's been a few months since God taught me that lesson and I've shared it with hundreds of women who have been convicted about their daily choices. But most of all, there hasn't been a day since then, that God hasn't reminded me to "close the door" when I even start back down the path of negative thinking. I'm so very grateful for the way he has ingrained this truth in my heart and mind.

HAVE I CLOSED THE DOOR?

Just why is it so hard for me
To keep that old door closed?
Why do I want to open it
And have my heart exposed?

You see, through God, I've shut the door
On words that caused such pain,
So why go back and open it
And in that pain remain?

I've also closed the door on fear
That God's plan wasn't best.
So when I go back through that door
It fills me with unrest.

I've closed the door, I won't return
For this is my new choice,
And when I'm tempted to turn back
I'll listen to God's voice.

Oh Lord, please keep me walking straight
Not turning back around,
Please help me see that trusting You
Is where my peace is found.

Carol Hopson

PERSONAL CHECKUP

If living for self:

Your first thought might be "Why is this happening to me?

Your second thought might be "What can I get out of this?"

Your third thought might be "This isn't fun and I don't like it!"

Your last thought might be "I guess God's plan doesn't work for me."

If living for God:

Your first thought might be "It's not my choice but I'll trust God!"

Your second thought might be "I need to see what verses might help me though this."

Your third thought might be "I wonder how I can grow to be more like Christ through this?"

Your last thought might be "I hope God will use this for His glory."

Bible Study Questions for Chapter 4 are on page 135.

CHAPTER 5

From Surviving to Thriving

Do you ever feel like you're on a merry-go-round that just keeps going and you can't get off? You're just hanging on and trying to survive. You probably wouldn't call this kind of living "fun" or what you had hoped for, but it's where you are. Well, there's good news. God has provided a way for us to truly thrive in this life, no matter what our circumstances are.

I was far away from home, in a foreign country, with a ten-hour time difference. By God's grace, I was giving six messages and counseling all hours of the day and night. The problem was that my body didn't like the time change and didn't adjust to it...ever! I'd go to my cold, lonely room, with no radio or TV, no one to talk to and then would lay awake for the entire night, knowing I would have to get up and be God's messenger and servant for another eighteen hours. I began to wonder how I would survive.

But as I laid in bed on the third sleepless night, God opened my eyes to a very precious truth. This was all a part of His plan for me or it wouldn't be happening. God's training was for me right then, not when I got the sleep I thought I needed. His purpose was that I totally trust and submit to Him and see these nights as part of my journey of growth with my loving Savior. I needed to see them as times to thrive and not just survive. I began to read all the Scriptures I could find on rest and discovered over and over that God gives us rest...not necessarily sleep.

The Lord your God gives you rest...
(Joshua 1:13)

Rest in the Lord and wait patiently for Him.
(Psalm 37:7)

Come unto me all who are weary and heavy-laden and I will give you rest.
(Matthew 11;28)

To move from surviving to thriving, I had to believe that God would give me rest, even if I had no sleep, because rest comes from Him. Then I began to read the verses about strength and found the same thing; we aren't just strengthened by eight hours of sleep, God says He gives strength to the weary.

God is our refuge and strength, a very present ~~*i*~~
in trouble.

(Psalm 46

The Lord stood with me and strengthened me...
(2 Timothy 4:17a)

He gives strength to the weary, and to him who
lacks might, He increases power.

(Isaiah 40:29)

I certainly fit into that category and so I asked sovereign God to give strength for the day ahead to His weary child, and requested that He would increase His power in me. And then I read,

...Whoever serves, let him do so as by the strength
which God supplies; so that in all things God may
be glorified through Jesus Christ...

(1 Peter 4:11)

I was getting excited now, I knew that God wanted to teach me a new depth of His sufficiency and my inadequacy and I was eager to learn. I realized that the sleepless nights were what God wanted to use for His glory, and so I willingly submitted to it, studied His word throughout the night and began my days with renewed strength. Each morning I was greeted by many who inquired "How did you sleep?" as I'm often asked at retreats. And each time I'd say with a big smile, "I slept as much as God wanted me to and I'm ready for the day." No one knew that I was not sleeping at all until the end of the retreat when I shared how God had helped me thrive on His strength alone. They could hardly believe it as they said I never even looked tired and thought I must be getting plenty of rest.

ˈetreat was over and we were on the
returned sleep to me but I had learned
ꞮꞮꞮꞮꞮꞮꞮꞮꞮus than gold.

Hebrews 12:1-3, NLT:

*everything that hinders us, as well
as ꞮꞮꞮꞮ ꞱꞱꞱꞱ h dogs at our feet, and let us run the
race that we have to run with patience, our eyes
fixed on Jesus the source and the goal of our faith.
For He Himself endured a cross and thought nothing of its shame because of the joy He knew would
follow His suffering, and He is now seated at the
right hand of God's throne. Think constantly of
Him enduring all that sinful men could say
against Him and you will not lose your purpose or
your courage.*

It's important to note that the word "race" here is
agnone in the Greek from which we get our word "agony".
In other words, this Christian life, this race, is often ago-
nizing, but with God's help and power, we can run it with
patient endurance and truly thrive. However, we need to
see life as a marathon, not a sprint. Too often, I've looked
at situations in my life as short sprints and I'm trying to
reach the goal of circumstances changing or having things
feel better. For instance, I've been faced with the possibil-
ity of cancer more than once and have had to wait through
months of testing to know what I was facing, I was tempted to think, when this is over, I'll be so happy but I just
have to get through this. That is sort of sprinting toward
the desired goal but it is not walking by faith and seeing
each day as the journey that God has planned for me. I
found that in those waiting weeks, God wanted to use me

many times to share His love with a nurse, a doctor, a fellow patient in the waiting room and others.

To thrive and grow, I need to run with endurance, realizing that this life is a marathon, not a sprint. So let's look at some of the requirements for marathon runners. First of all, running in a marathon requires freedom, or the lack of weight or heavy clothes. You never see marathon runners wearying heavy sweats or weights around their ankles. They want to carry as little extra weight as possible. In the above verses, we are instructed to do the same thing spiritually. We are told to "strip off everything that hinders us, as well as the sin which dogs at our feet".

What do we need to strip off to be better prepared to run the race God has given us. Let me suggest a few things that weight us down:

♦ Fear, which is a complete lack of faith.

♦ Doubt about God's promises or plan for our lives or our children's lives.

♦ Bitterness because of an unresolved hurt in our lives.

♦ Discontent with what God is allowing.

♦ Self exaltation because I think I know better than God.

♦ Unbelief, which is the root of all the above weights.

To strip off these is to confess that they are sin and ask God to help us live without those heavy weights so that we have the freedom to thrive in our walk and relationship with Him. Did you notice how the Scripture says, "the sin which dogs at our feet"? That is such a vivid picture of an irritating, yapping dog that just keeps nipping at your ankles, causing great frustration. The weights mentioned above are like that; if not left in the Father's hands, they will continually irritate us and cause us to sin.

A marathon also requires patience. My daughter was a distance runner and I was continually impressed at the difference in a distance runner and a sprinter. The sprinters were finished in a flash with quick glory or defeat, but she continually had to pace herself, strengthen herself and stay emotionally ready for the distance. In order to strengthen myself for this life's journey, I need to understand the following things about God which will give me the needed patience to run victoriously.

God is in control even when it doesn't feel like it! Romans 8:28

God will see me through this marathon as I let Him be my trainer. Philippians 1:6

God has a purpose for everything He allows in my life. James 1:2-4

God does not work on my time schedule. Psalm 31:14-15

God will constantly guide my steps as I submit to Him. Psalm 32:8

God will use me as I steadfastly follow Him.
1 Corinthians 15:58

If I truly believe what God has promised, I can then patiently wait for Him to work out His plan for me and for those I love.

A marathon also requires a goal. Can you imagine a marathon runner who has no goal in mind....just endless running with no end, no reward, no rest? The discouragement would be overwhelming and quitting would seem like the best plan. Let me ask you something, "If you were to die today what would others say was your greatest priority? Would it be work, your family, keeping your body in shape, making more money?" There is nothing wrong with these things, but none of them should be our main goal. Again, we must go to God's Word for our goal, *"Let your light so shine before men that they may see your good works and glorify your Father who is in heaven."* In other words, all that we do in our homes, our jobs, our ministries, our free time, should be with the purpose of being a light by which others are drawn to the Lord. That is what makes living truly worthwhile.

I was once again going to get my hair cut and "touched up" and knew that I needed to ask God to make this a profitable time, for His glory, even if I didn't feel like spending that time in the beauty parlor. I prayed on my way there that if God had someone who needed encouragement or needed to know about Him, that I would be available and aware. While sitting in my chair and waiting for the coloring to take, I began writing in my notes about what God had been teaching me. I felt I needed to write a poem about "Closing the Door" to Satan's attacks since God had given me such a vivid picture of that, as mentioned in a previous chapter.

I sat there writing and someone walked right up to me and said, "What are you writing?" which should have surprised me, but it didn't. I have found that when you tell God you're available and ask Him to use you, He does! So, with drippy, ugly hair, I smiled and said, "I'm writing a poem about how to close the door on all of Satan's attacks on my life." This person looked at me in amazement and said, "You know how to do that?" I replied that I didn't always do it, but I knew how to do it. She asked me to read my poem to her and explain what it meant, which I was delighted to do. When I was finished, she asked me how I could possibly have known how much she needed that right now. I told her that I didn't know, but God did and I had asked Him to show me someone who needed His love or encouragement before I came in that day. She began to weep, I prayed with her and she said she was going to go to her car and spend time getting her life straightened out with the Lord and close that door that she had opened so wide. Praise the Lord for His loving kindness and faithfulness.

PERSONAL CHECKUP

If only surviving:

You'll feel depressed throughout the day and you don't know why.

You'll have a difficult time beginning your day.

You won't find joy in the little things.

You'll be easily annoyed with others and all you have to do.

Life will seem overwhelming and unfruitful.

If desiring to thrive: (by God's grace)

You'll feel anticipation as you awake to a new day.

You'll know that you will always face some difficult days, but will also know that God will see you through everything you encounter.

You'll seek opportunities to share God's love in your everyday life.

You'll truly believe that joy comes from living in light of God's principles and from being obedient to His Word.

Bible Study Questions for Chapter 5 are on page 139.

CHAPTER 6

From Alarmed to Assured

You've just received news that has shaken you to the core. Someone has died, or they've found cancer in your tests, or your child has gone back on drugs. Of course, you're alarmed...you're human. But where do you go from there? Do you stay alarmed, fearful and distraught or do you find assurance in your knowledge of God's love for you and His plan for your life, whether you understand it or not?

When I heard the car screech to a halt in front of our house, followed by a scream, I was alarmed. I ran out to find my 3-year-old daughter lying beneath the front bumper of a car. The driver and his wife were panicked beyond words and the driver kept saying, "I killed her, I killed her!" It seemed like the whole neighborhood had come out to see what had transpired. As I was running out my front door, somehow knowing that it was my daughter who had been hit, my loving Lord spoke to me and reminded me to not be afraid because He was right there with me. It gave me a miraculous peace, which I desperately needed to deal with the situation. The driver was panicked, his wife was sobbing and there was no 911 to call back then. I shouted to my neighbor to take care of my 5-year-old son and we put my daughter in the car of the people who had run into her. I held her in my lap in the back seat while they drove and sobbed. She didn't make a sound but she was breathing.

The Lord whispered to me to stay calm and try to comfort the couple in the front seat. I kept telling them that Jennifer was in God's hands and I was trusting Him so they shouldn't worry, just get us to the hospital. Of course, we had no cell phones back then so I had to wait until my daughter was admitted before I could call my husband and let him know what had happened. It wasn't until he arrived at the hospital that I let down and shed some tears. God had so greatly upheld me with His strength and love. While we waited for the doctor to bring us the news, we were able to share with that dear couple, how God gives peace to His children and how our lives are in His hands. They were so ready to listen. God had another miracle in store; though Jennifer had been hit head-on, she had no broken bones, just a mild concussion and some scratches and bruises. It totally amazed the doctors and the frightened couple who waited with us.

Let me just share one more thing about this incident. I had been having Good News Clubs in my home for seven years in that neighborhood. A Good News Club is like Vacation Bible School in your home. I felt God wanted me to have this club in my home on every Friday, after school, so that I could reach the neighborhood children for Christ. I had visited each home of each child who had accepted Christ in that club. Now, God had allowed this accident to happen and all the mothers in the neighborhood were watching to see how "this Christian" would react. I didn't know all this at the time, but they shared it with me later and it gave me so many opportunities to share about the peace God had given me and how I felt His presence with me throughout the whole ordeal. They definitely wanted to know more about this personal relationship with my Savior and I was very happy to share it with them.

God's Word says,

> *Consider it a sheer gift, friends, when tests and challenges come at you from all sides. You know that under pressure, your faith-life is forced into the open and shows its true colors. So don't try to get out of anything prematurely. Let it do its work so you become mature and well-developed, not deficient in any way.*
>
> (James 1:2-4, The Message)

I truly believe that God was using this "accident" to force my faith-life out into the open so that my neighbors could see it and He was helping me grow and mature in Him through the process.

Alarming times are opportunities to be aware of God's presence and then be assured of His loving care for us. But we usually don't see our trials as opportunities, so it's important to see how that is possible. The passage goes on to say in verses 5-7, *The Message*,

> *If you don't know what you're doing, pray to the Father. He loves to help. You'll get His help, and won't be condescended to when you ask for it. Ask boldly, believingly, without a second thought. People who worry their prayers are like wind-whipped waves. Don't think you're going to get anything from the Master that way, adrift at sea, keeping your options open.*

I can't explain to you how it works, I can just tell you that when I asked God to give me a calm assurance of His presence, He did! And when I asked for His peace, He gave it, miraculously! Then He used it all for His glory.

To go from alarm to assurance in any situation, I believe we need to truly know our Shepherd. Let's think about one of the most well-known passages in our Bible which is Psalm 23:1, *"The Lord is my Shepherd, I shall not want."* We've all quoted it many times, heard it read at funerals and probably memorized it; but is it true that we have no wants because we know the Shepherd? One small child was quoting this to her mommy and said, "The Lord is my Shepherd, I've got all I want!" What a great interpretation from a child. Did you know that God calls us His sheep, and sheep are known to be fearful, defenseless, directionless, dependent and easily distracted. In fact, shepherds tell us that sheep only rest when they are free from fear, conflict and irritations. They simply will not lie down and rest if they sense any danger. They also have a "butting order" from which we get our term "butting in". There is usually an arrogant, cunning, domineering old ewe who will boss any bunch of sheep and drive them away from the best grazing and resting areas. There are also rams who get "rambunctious" in mating season and want to show off and butt others. This causes sheep to be edgy and irritated and they won't rest or eat and will actually lose weight.

How does a shepherd change all of this? How do the sheep finally eat, sleep and rest? It all changes when the shepherd comes into view. The arrogant and irritating sheep stop their behavior because they know the shepherd will take control and the others rest for the same reason. They know that the shepherd is the one who feeds them, comforts them, directs them, heals them and lays down his life for them, and so they trust him to take care of everything. It all gets down to their awareness of the shepherd's presence.

> *I am the good Shepherd; and I know my own and my own know Me, even as the Father knows Me and I know the Father and I lay down My life for the sheep.*
>
> (John 10:14-15)

To be assured that what God is allowing in my life has passed through His hand, I must remember that He is the only One who has met all my needs...salvation, forgiveness, acceptance, feeding, purpose, comfort, a future, healing and so much more. The reason we stay alarmed or fearful at times is that we've lost sight of our Shepherd. I remember an incident when my husband and I arrived at a school function where there was dissension and uneasiness. Now my husband, the headmaster of the school at the time, had silver hair, a calming presence, a soothing voice, a love for those present and was someone that most everyone trusted. I shall never forget the words of one woman as she saw him walk in, "Oh, Mr. Hopson is here! Now everything will be fine and we can all relax." Just the presence of someone she trusted, who had authority, brought peace to her heart, even before anything changed. That's the way it is with our personal Shepherd. Just the sight of Him, in our thoughts, our prayers, our scripture reading, our meditating, can and should bring that peace to our hearts, because He is the true authority, the trusted One, the miracle worker who says,

> *Do not fear for I am with you, do not anxiously look about you, for I am your God. I will strengthen you, surely I will help you, surely I will uphold you with my righteous right hand.*
>
> (Isaiah 41:10)

In reading the book entitled *Extreme Devotion* by the Voice of the Martyrs, I came across the following story from Indonesia.

> Fritz felt each crashing blow to his head and prayed for strength. The Muslim attackers surrounded him and took turns beating him in the face. One of the Muslim attackers brandished a large knife thinking this would rid them of the Christian pastor. The first time the blade went into Fritz, all he could do was yell, "Jesus!" He was stabbed repeatedly. And each time, he yelled, "Jesus!" The attackers grew frustrated at the pastor who just wouldn't die.

The radical Muslims proceeded to pull the benches and pulpit from the church and set them on fire. Two of the Muslims grabbed Fritz and heaved him onto the blazing wood. Satisfied with their attack, they ran away. Fritz doesn't remember much after that, but he knows one thing. Not a hair on his head was singed. Shortly after the attack, Fritz was brought to the largest hospital in that area of Indonesia but he was refused treatment when they learned he was a Christian. He was brought to another hospital, but the attending doctor said that if he happened to live through the night, he would have permanent brain damage.

After a long recovery, Fritz is now preaching again at a new church. To his amazement, one of the Muslims who attacked Fritz began looking for him, only to ask a single question; "Who is Jesus?"

My eyes were misty as I read this. I thought of the many times I've questioned what God was doing instead of just crying out in faith, "Jesus!" He is the answer and He is where we find comfort, peace and purpose and by trusting Him completely, we put "feet" to our faith. The next time you are alarmed by something you hear or experience, ask yourself, "What can I be assured of from God's Word in this situation? How does God's presence bring me comfort and how might God want to bring my "faith-life" to light for others to see?"

My second granddaughter, Becca, was in love with Barney, the TV character. Knowing this, I had purchased a darling book about Barney and couldn't wait for her to visit so that I could read it to her. She curled up on my lap and with delight, I began to read to her. The book was about

71

Barney on the farm and so I was telling her that Barney was feeding the cows, and then I'd ask, "Becca, what does the cow say?" I knew she could tell me in her darling little voice and I was eager to hear it. (Nana's are like that.) But, Becca just looked at the picture of Barney, touched him with her chubby little hand and said, "Barney". Oh well, I tried the next page, "Becca, what does the duck say?" And again, with the most loving voice, little Becca would touch Barney on that page and say "Baaaaarney" in a long drawn-out way, to emphasize her affection. This happened on every page in the book. I couldn't get her to make any of the adorable animal sounds that I knew she could say. Finally, Becca put her little hands on my cheeks and turned my head to face her and said, "Nana, I dos (just) see Barney!!" In other words, nothing else mattered to her. Her eyes were fixed on the one she loved.

Since then, I've tried to practice that in my love relationship with Jesus. When other things seek to distract me, I try to say, "I just see Jesus!"

PERSONAL CHECKUP

If you're easily alarmed:

You quickly say, "Why me?" when difficult circumstances arise.

You will focus on the problem day and night.

You are fearful and unable to sleep because of your worries.

You won't look for ways to exhibit God's grace in your life.

You'll readily complain to others of how unfair life is.

If you're assured of God's presence and love:

You'll try to quickly move from alarm to faith in God's Word and His plan.

You'll seek God's help in dealing with the situation in a way that honors Him.

You'll show your "faith-life" in the midst of your trials.

You'll seek prayerful counsel and support from Godly friends.

You'll have an inward peace, even when you can't see any resolution.

Bible Study Questions for Chapter 6 are on page 143.

CHAPTER 7

From Stumbling Blocks to Stepping Stones

A crowd had gathered around the man who was sculpting something out of a huge piece of marble. None of them could figure out what he was creating. They kept watching him chisel away and finally, one brave soul interrupted his concentration and asked, "Excuse me sir, but what are you making?" "A horse" was his reply. Well, she couldn't see anything that looked like a horse at this point and so she asked, "How will you make that huge piece of marble look like a horse?" He simply replied, " I just chisel away everything that doesn't look like a horse!"

When I heard this story, it seemed that the Lord was saying to me, "Carol, you may see things in your life as 'stumbling blocks' because you don't understand the process. But what I'm doing is chiseling away all the things in your life that don't resemble Me. They are actually 'stepping stones' to help you become more Christ-like." What a dramatic change this had made in my thinking. Since then, I've asked God to help me recognize His chiseling and not fight it or resent it, but see it as a part of His loving purpose for my life. Of course I haven't always welcomed the chisel. But, it is my hearts desire to try to see things from God's perspective, rather than my own.

When my husband was suddenly out of work and we were in a state far away from family and friends, the situation seemed like a huge stumbling block. We didn't know why God would allow this to happen when we have moved in obedience to His call. We didn't know how we were going to live or make our monthly house payments. We didn't know if my husband could find another job due to his age and type of work. We didn't have family around to support or comfort us. We felt alone and sometimes forgotten by God. All of these things certainly don't sound like stepping stones, but they were. As we offered our worries, our days, our future and our lives up to God on a daily basis, He gave us new insights into Scriptures we had known all of our lives and reminded us of how life-giving His promises were. But, one of the biggest stepping stones was that through this change of plans, God moved me to write my story down in my first book called, "But God, This Wasn't My Plan!" Before this, I had never planned to write a book but God so clearly instructed me to begin writing and He has kept me writing ever since. God has used the written words He gave me to minister to thousands and they have reached all over the world to encourage, challenge and edify believers, by His grace alone. This manuscript is the eighth book God has brought out of the "stumbling blocks" turned into "stepping stones" in my life. Without the great disappointment of the loss of my husband's job, the major illnesses, the unexpected changes, the feeling of helplessness and the grace of God in my life, I believe that these books would never have been written. To God be the glory for all of it!

Let me share how others have turned much more difficult situations into stepping stones...for God's glory.

I was about an hour from home and was finished with my errand. As I headed out of the shopping center, my eyes were drawn towards a large restaurant. As I drove by it I kept thinking that I should go inside, but I really wasn't hungry and had a long drive ahead of me. Still, I had this tug in my heart to stop and go inside at 11:30 in the morning. Since I had asked God to use me that day for His glory and to be available to touch someone with His love, I couldn't ignore this strong pull. So, I parked the car and walked inside. It was dark and empty and the waiter said, "One for lunch?" I replied, "I guess so." He sat me in a small booth in the corner where I proceeded to order a cup of soup, since I wasn't really hungry. I had not been sitting there five minutes when a beautiful young waitress came up to my table and said, "I can't believe you're here!" I looked at her in amazement and asked her why she said that. She sat down on the other side of the booth and began telling me her story. She told me that she had wanted to talk with me for six months but didn't know how to find me and now here I was, sitting in the restaurant where she worked. Here is what she shared with me:

She had gone to a retreat where I was speaking a couple of years ago. She came from a very dysfunctional home with alcoholic parents but she had recently accepted Christ as her Savior. The problem was that she didn't know what to do from there and felt helpless with her younger brother and sister who were still in that home. Someone invited her to a church retreat and so she went. The retreat theme was "From Ordinary to Extraordinary Living" and was all about what God can and will do in our lives when we tell Him we're available for Him to use. I shared what it really meant to be available to God and why we are called to be God's ambassadors each day. (2 Corinthians 5:20) I told several stories of the miracles I had experienced when I've been available and aware that God wanted me to be His light.

Well, this young lady, just out of college, took all of this to heart and when she got home she prayed and told God she was available to win her young brother and sister to the Lord if He would just show her what to do. She said that she kept saying to the Lord, "I'm available!" whenever she would think of her young siblings. Then one day while she was praying, God put it on her heart to write a devotional booklet for her sister who was just starting high school. She related to me that she had made so many poor choices in high school because she didn't know any better and was afraid her sister would do the same. So, she decided to study her Bible and write out one hundred verses that she thought would be helpful to her 13-year-old sister and then she would write out how each one would have helped her during those years. Are you as shocked as I was? Here is this new, young Christian writing a devotional journal to help her little sister...amazing! Anyway, she wrote the journal and gave it to her sister who was just entering high school. She asked her to please read one every day. At first, her sister didn't seem to respond very much but half way through the journal, she was ready to have her big sister help her receive Christ as her Savior. Praise to Almighty God!

Now, she told God she was available to help her rather wild junior high brother come to the Lord but she didn't know how. She prayed and decided that if she could get him to a Christian youth camp, maybe he would become a Christian too. She talked to her alcoholic parents about it and they said they wouldn't pay a dime for such a waste of time. So, she worked and earned enough money to pay her brother's way to camp. This was on top of all her other expenses. When it came time for him to go, the parents wouldn't let him attend unless she went with him, so she got off work and went to the week long camp as a counselor. And guess what, He gave his life to the Lord that week at camp! Now all three kids were believers and wanted to live for the Lord. I was blurry-eyed and had goose bumps and was sitting on the edge of my seat. She finished by telling me that she had asked God to help her find me so she could tell me what God had done when she simply said, "I'm available!" and then she smiled broadly and said, "and He brought you right to me!" Now, she wanted to meet with me again and find out how to continue growing in her new walk with the Lord.

This precious young lady used all the stumbling blocks of being raised by alcoholic parents, never feeling loved or secure, making huge mistakes in her teen years...and she allowed God to turn them into stepping stones to bring her brother and sister to Christ.

> *And this is the confidence which we have before Him, that, if we ask anything according to His will, He hears us.*
>
> (1 John 5:14)

Again I'm reminded that we are called "sheep" in the Scriptures for a specific reason. When we're faced with changes, a new direction or something unknown, we often see it as a mistake or a stumbling block. But Psalm 23 tells us that the Lord, our Shepherd "leads us in the paths of righteousness for His names' sake." Shepherds tell us that sheep will follow the same path or trail over and over and never leave their comfort zone. They will stay in the same worn ruts, they will eat every bit of nourishment in that path and actually starve if not led to "new pastures". Also, the path or pasture will become infested with parasites, which can also destroy the flock. I've learned that one of the most important aspects of tending a flock is to continually seek out new pasture and keep the flock on the move. This is for the health and well being of the sheep. How often have you looked at the "new pastures" in your life as something God is providing for your growth, nourishment and health?

Isaiah 53:6 tells us that:

> *All we like sheep have gone astray, and have turned every one to his own way...*

In other words, we want to do our own thing and go our own way when we're not living by faith and we miss what God is trying to show us.

Through the many moves and changed plans in my life, God has graciously shown me that great growth and opportunities come from moving on to "new pastures". I haven't always wanted them or chosen them, but they have always been for my good and for the glory of my Heavenly Father. You see, Psalm 23:3 goes on to say that:

He guides me in the paths of righteousness for His name's sake.

He leads me in new paths to honor and glorify His name. An unhealthy flock of sheep is a shame to the shepherd who tends it so they want to keep their sheep on the move and thriving. The shepherd guides his flock to new places of HIS choosing. In the same way, our great Shepherd keeps providing "stepping stones" to maturity and spiritual health for "His name's sake". I love looking at my new seasons or opportunities in this light. They are no longer stumbling blocks, but stepping stones, provided by my Shepherd's loving heart.

Remember the man who was chiseling on that huge piece of marble to create a horse? Is God doing some chiseling in your life right now? Are you willing to let Him turn your hurts, your disappointments and your new seasons into stepping stones...for His name's sake?

YOU'RE CHISELING AGAIN, LORD!

You're chiseling again, dear Lord
And I can feel the pain
It seems there's always so much work
That in me still remains

Just when I think I'm doing great
And life is sailing on
I feel the cut of the sculptor's knife
And lose my joy and song

Why do you need to work so hard
On one small child like me?
Could I just have a week of joy
Or maybe two or three?

Oh yes, I know your answer Lord
And why Your work goes on
It isn't to discourage me
Or rob my joy and song

Your chiseling work continues on
It's what your love must do
You're taking off the ugly parts
That don't resemble You!

Carol Hopson

PERSONAL CHECKUP:

If seeing things as stumbling blocks:

You'll look at daily interruptions with irritability.

You'll be frustrated at the changed plans in your life.

You'll complain to others about how you've been hurt or wronged.

You'll miss some of the greatest growth opportunities God has for you.

If seeing things as stepping stones:

You'll look for God's hand in everything.

You'll quickly recognize your negative spirit and confess it.

You'll ask God to show you how to use your situation as a stepping stone.

You'll yield yourself and your day to the Lord, to do as He pleases.

Bible Study Questions for Chapter 7 are on page 147.

CHAPTER 8

From Feeling to Kneeling

Do any of these statements sound familiar to you?

But God, this isn't fair!

But God, I'm tired of waiting!

But God, this isn't what I expected in life!

But God, I don't think I can handle this!

But God, I'm too tired to carry on!

But God, You're not answering my prayers!

Of course they do or you wouldn't be human. The problem is that we need to take the feeling and turn it into kneeling...quickly! Let's look at why God calls us His sheep again to understand the need for kneeling before the Shepherd. In Psalm 23 we read that the good Shepherd *"anoints my head with oil..."* In studying the shepherds care of his sheep, I've found that this is a very important element of their relationship. The oil was used for three purposes. First of all, it was applied to each sheep's head to keep flies and insects from laying eggs in their nostrils and to repel them from irritating their eyes. Sheep could get so distraught from this type of irritation in their noses that they would bang their head against a tree until they did great harm to themselves. Secondly, the oil was used to heal their wounds and soothe them. And lastly, it was put on the heads or horns of sheep who were rambunctious so that their horns would just slip off each other in a fight and they wouldn't injure each other.

Now let's see why we, God's sheep, need to be anointed with the oil of God's Word. First of all, as we apply the truths from the Bible, it prevents the irritations in our lives from taking over.

> *My dear brothers and sisters, be quick to listen, slow to speak and slow to get angry. Your anger can never make things right in God's sight...and remember, it is a message to obey, not just to listen to.*
>
> (James 1:19,20 & 22a, NLT)

Let me just tell you that as my husband's administrative assistant for fifteen years in the Christian school we founded, I was always the front line of attack for anyone with a complaint about a teacher, a grade, a playground incident or anything else that came up. Those were some of the most challenging days for me to be "quick to listen, slow to speak and slow to get angry." When I didn't apply this "oil" of God's Word, I would lose my patience and say things I would later regret. If I did apply the "oil", I would hold my tongue, listen patiently and let God control my speech and actions. Having God's Word in my heart and on my desk in front of me, soothed and convicted me many times and helped me pass on God's grace to others.

Sheep need oil to heal their wounds and so do we as God's children. I had been so deeply hurt by someone that I had loved and trusted and couldn't understand this person's change of heart. The cruel words were so unfair and I couldn't believe how deeply betrayed I felt. I had poured so much love into this person for so long and none of it made sense. The pain was overwhelming until I applied the "oil" of God's precious word. God so clearly comforted me with these healing words,

> *This suffering is all part of what God has called*
> *you to. Christ, who suffered for you, is your exam-*
> *ple. Follow in his steps. He never sinned, and he*
> *never deceived anyone. He did not retaliate when*
> *he was insulted. When he suffered, he did not*
> *threaten to get even. He left his case in the hands*
> *of God, who always judges fairly.*
> (1 Peter 2:21-23, NLT)

Here is what I think is the most important aspect of the shepherd applying oil to his sheep. In order for the oil to be applied, the sheep had to come to the shepherd, stand still before him, lower their heads and submit to the shepherd's hands. Remember that this chapter is about feeling or kneeling. When I'm acting on my feelings, I will always make wrong choices and will not be lowering my head in submission before the Shepherd. But when I come to the Shepherd, kneel before Him in humility and submit to His loving, guiding hands, I will then make right choices that will honor Him.

Humble yourselves therefore, under the mighty hand of God, that He may exalt you at the proper time, casting all your anxiety upon Him because He cares for you.

(1 Peter 5:6-7)

And again we are reminded that:

God is opposed to the proud, but gives grace to the humble. Submit therefore to God...

(James 4:6b & 7a)

In Psalm 42:11 we read David's cry,

Why are you cast down my soul? And why art thou disquieted within me, hope in God.

The word "cast" down here might refer to a "cast" sheep. This is a sheep who has stumbled or fallen and has turned over on his back and he can't get up again by himself. If the shepherd doesn't find him soon, he could die because predators such as buzzards, vultures or coyotes know that a "cast" sheep is easy prey. The shepherd is always keeping track of his flock and searches out any that are lost and when he finds a "cast" sheep he gently turns the sheep back on his side. Then he slowly lifts him to his feet and begins to rub his limbs to restore circulation. He will hold the little lamb or sheep up and quietly talk to him with encouraging words while waiting for him to regain his strength. Oh how I love this picture of the shepherd and his sheep because it is a beautiful picture of how my Shepherd lovingly restores me, especially when I've felt "cast down" by many circumstances. "Your promise revives me, it comforts me in all my troubles."

I will never forget your commandments, for you have used them to restore my joy and health.
(Psalm 119:50 & 93, NLT)

Another incident in my life, reminds me of the importance of kneeling. Oh, what a horrible "feeling" I woke up with on a Friday morning! I was due to leave for a retreat in one hour and I had the worst pinched nerve in my neck and couldn't move my head without great pain. "Oh no Lord, this can't be your plan for me when I'm going to speak for You! Could it?" My dear husband massaged my neck, we iced it, heated it and tried everything we knew to do. I had to leave for the airport soon so we prayed and asked God to remove the pain so that I could minister that weekend. After the drive to the airport, the pain was as strong as ever and I couldn't straighten up my neck or turn my head. My husband prayed for me again as he got ready to leave me at the airport and I knew that God wanted me to leave my feelings with Him and truly kneel before Him, allowing Him to do His work in me and through me...despite the unfairness, the pain, the lack of understanding, or the healing I desired etc.

I dragged my suitcase into the airport and after getting my boarding pass, I proceeded to the security check line. When it came time for me to lift my suitcase up on to the conveyer belt, I couldn't do it because of the pain. The kind lady behind me lifted it up for me. I thanked her profusely and then she helped me lift it down at the other end. How kind she was! I walked on to my waiting area and finding no one there, sat down and rested my head against the wall. As I sat there, I prayed and asked God if He would somehow use this pain for His glory if He chose not to remove it.

I had not been sitting there more than two or three minutes when I felt a body sit down right beside me. My eyes were closed, there was no one else waiting in this area and yet, someone sat practically on top of me. Why? I wondered. I opened my eyes to see the woman who had helped me with my luggage. I smiled at her and greeted her again. She said, "I just have to know why you are traveling when you're obviously in so much pain?" I replied to her that I was going to speak to a group of women and tell them how to have peace in any situation they face. She looked at me in amazement and said, "You know how to do that?" I told her that I did and with that she began to cry. She cried hard and I put my arms around her and told her that I thought God had sent me there to tell her that He loved and cared for her. I knew nothing of her problem until she finally said, "I've just been diagnosed with inoperable pancreatic cancer and they have given me no hope. I'm going back to say goodbye to my mother and sister. Can you really tell me how to find peace in this?"

Do you realize that just minutes before this, I had knelt before God and asked Him to use this stiff neck for His glory? Well, by God's providence and grace, I was able to spend the next forty minutes giving this dear woman the good news of the gospel, telling her of the assurance of forgiveness, a future in heaven and peace beyond understanding. She was a sponge, taking it all in, asking question after question. When we finally had to board the plane, she thanked me over and over and I hugged her and prayed for her and we each went our way. The stiff neck stayed with me the entire weekend but I was so humbled at how God used it in the airport and throughout the weekend. When I finally arrived back at the airport for my return flight, guess who found me again? Yes, the same woman was there to fly home and she shared that she had prayed and found peace with God and shared it with her family. Oh the joy of turning distraught feelings into kneeling before God and letting Him do His work.

> *Now the God of peace, who brought up from the dead the great Shepherd of the sheep through the blood of the eternal covenant, even Jesus our Lord, equip you in every good thing to do His will, working in us that which is pleasing in His sight, through Jesus Christ, to whom be the glory forever and ever, Amen.*
>
> (Hebrews 13:20-21)

PERSONAL CHECKUP

If you're living by feelings:

You will be easily discouraged by your circumstances.

You won't be open to the opportunities God has in your day.

You'll often feel that life isn't fair and God doesn't care about you.

Your feelings will affect your decisions, rather than God's truths affecting them.

If you're living by kneeling:

You'll take your emotions to the Lord and kneel before Him.

You won't worry about not understanding the "whys" in your life.

You'll see your disappointments as God's appointments and be ready to be used by Him.

You'll learn to enjoy the "kneeling" process because it takes all of the burden off of your shoulders.

Bible Study Questions for Chapter 8 are on page 149.

CHAPTER 9

From Stressed to Blessed

As I sat in the car on the last leg of my journey, I recalled all that God had done that past weekend. So many lives were changed forever...because of the Holy Spirit's work. I had just finished my eighth weekend retreat and was beginning the nine-hour journey home. Almost five of those hours were spent in the car, in heavy traffic, trying to get to the airport to fly home.

I was unusually tired because of the long hours of speaking, counseling and traveling and wanted so much to just put my head back and sleep those four or five hours away. Unfortunately, as it seemed to me, there were three others in the car who weren't doing so well themselves. The driver wasn't feeling well so asked her friend to drive. The new driver got carsick and kept stopping for fresh air and the third passenger, in the back seat with me, was terribly shy and suffered from such low self-esteem that I felt I needed to continually try to help and encourage her.

Everyone was feeling low and complaining and the car had a feeling of heaviness as we crept along in the heavy traffic. After such a wonderful, uplifting weekend, I just didn't think this was right, but I finally decided to close my eyes and try to rest for a few minutes. As I tried to relax, I was thinking, "Why me, Lord?" I'm the one who has been putting out so much this weekend. I'm the one who should be complaining about not feeling well as I've only had a few hours of sleep all weekend. What's wrong with them? Why can't I be in a car where everyone's happy and sharing all the good things about the retreat? You can see that I didn't have a great attitude and was thinking only of myself!

After about one half hour of trying to ignore their issues, the Lord finally got through to me. Here I was, the one who writes about God changing ordinary moments into extraordinary ones...the one who teaches that each moment we are called to be a light for Him...the one who says that joy comes when we accept God's plan and glorify Him in it...and I was not living what I taught and believed. So, I asked God to help me have a quick attitude adjustment and use the situation for His glory. I asked God to show me what I could do to change the atmosphere in the car and get my eyes off of myself. He led me to ask the weary, complaining travelers if they would like to hear a story. They thought that would be okay and so I began. God gave me story after story about His miraculous appointments when I had submitted to His plan and was available to share His love with others. One story was about a train ride, one was at a counter in a restaurant and one was about a walk on the beach. In each story, the main point was how much God loved the lost in this world and was drawing them to Christ through His servant.

I couldn't believe how the time flew by, and before long, we were at the airport. As I started to say my goodbyes, I noticed that each passenger was weeping and as each one said goodbye to me, they hugged me and thanked me for changing their vision from themselves to others. One said, "This was the best ride I've ever had!" Imagine that! God turned a carload of grumbling (including me) into a carload of gratitude!

> *My dear brothers and sisters, whenever trouble comes your way, let it be an opportunity for joy. For when your faith is tested, your endurance has a chance to grow. So let it grow, for when your endurance is fully developed, you will be strong in character and ready for anything.*
> (James 1:3-5, The Message)

You might think that this was the end of my story but it wasn't. I still had to wait in the airport for my delayed flight home. "Please Lord, could I just sleep on the plane? Could You possibly put an empty seat beside me so I don't feel the need to talk to someone about You?" (Selfish thought!)

I finally boarded the plane as one weary traveler who was anxious to see my husband and be home in my own bed again. As a young man approached and sat beside me, I greeted him pleasantly, asked a few questions and thought, "There, that was friendly enough, wasn't it Lord?" I thought I could now rest with a clear conscience. But, after about fifteen minutes of trying to ignore the person who was six inches from me, I felt the Lord urge me to try once again to see if he might be interested in hearing about God's love for him. I asked him what he did for a living and he told me about his computer business and seemed quite happy to talk about it. He then asked me what I did. I told him that I was a motivational speaker and author, knowing that this usually leads to another question. When he asked, "What kind of motivational speaker are you?" I thought, "Here we go, Lord!"

As I shared that I was a Christian who sought to motivate others to love and serve the Lord wholeheartedly, he began asking question after question about why I did that, how I got started, did people really change etc. Since I had been speaking that weekend about "Peace in the Midst of your Circumstances" he wanted to know how you could have that kind of peace. He also asked about each book I had written and seemed genuinely interested. What a great door God had opened for me!

Therefore be careful how you walk...making the most of your time, because the days are evil.
(Ephesians 5:15-16)

This dear young man repeated several times that he really didn't need any one to help him, he was doing fine on his own, and yet he kept asking questions and listening intently. At one point I said, "I'm only sharing this because I love the Lord so much and care deeply that others know how much God loves them. But, if you'd like me to just be quiet, I'll definitely respect that, so just let me know." He had moved to the United States from Germany five years before and had come across a few Christians in his field. He basically thought that each person could figure out his or her own way to knowing God. I asked him if he believed the Bible. He said that he believed parts of it or most of it; then, after pausing, he said that he probably thought all of it was true. To this I replied. "Did you know that the Bible states that there is only one way to know God and that is through accepting His Son, Jesus, and the price He paid for our sins on the cross?" I continued by asking him why God would send His only Son to die that horrible death on the cross if we could be forgiven from our sins and find true peace another way. That seemed to really puzzle him and he didn't reply.

By now the plane was landing and our time was running out. (My, this trip went fast!) He got out his pen and paper and began writing. I asked him what he was writing and he told me he wanted to write down some of the things I had told him and some of the verses I shared so he could look them up later. I was shocked! I'm always amazed at the power and presence of God in those situations. He also asked that I write down the titles of my books so he could look them up and then we exchanged e-mail addresses. He actually thanked me for not being pushy about my faith but said he was really glad that I had shared God's love with him. He then told me that his mother had been praying for him for many years and he was going to tell her about who

97

God had put next to him on the plane. Oh, how God honors the faithful prayers of mothers!

As the plane landed and we were getting our luggage down, I realized that I hadn't asked him his name. "I'm sorry, but I didn't get your name and I'd like to pray for you if that's okay with you." He looked me in the eye and he actually blushed. (It was easy to see because of his light German complexion.) "You're going to love this!" he said. "My name is Christian!" As we walked up the ramp to the terminal, he thanked me again and we parted ways. My very long "stressful" journey had been truly "blessed" by God.

I may have done the planting and Apollos the watering, but it was God who made the seed grow. The planter and waterer are nothing compared with Him who gives life to the seed.
(1 Corinthians 3:6-7, Phillips)

Forgive me Lord, for all the times I've been too stressed and missed being blessed by your best plan for me. Please help me say with David,

I will bless the Lord at all times; His praise shall continually be in my mouth. My soul shall make its boast in the Lord; the humble shall hear it and rejoice, O magnify the Lord with me, and let us exalt His name together.
(Psalm 34:1-3)

ONE OF THOSE DAYS

Today was one of those days
When everything went wrong.
Nothing went as I had planned
My day seemed oh so long!

No one came with words of cheer
To brighten up my day.
Just the opposite was true
Their problems on me lay.

But this day was so different
I didn't fume or fret
The tension in me didn't rise
And break out in cold sweat.

Yes, today was one of those days
When everything went wrong.
But I gave it to Jesus
And He blessed me all day long!

Carol Hopson

PERSONAL CHECKUP

If living with stress:

Your shoulders and neck will be tight.

You'll lash out easily when confronted with a different opinion.

You'll alienate others because you've lost your joy.

You'll miss so many opportunities to show God's grace to others.

If living as blessed:

You will want to outwardly praise God no matter what.

You'll see God at work because you're looking for His leading in your life.

You'll ask God to help you turn grumbling into gratitude.

You'll experience a deep joy because of your unhindered fellowship with the Lord.

Bible Study Questions for Chapter 9 are on page 153.

CHAPTER 10

From Delaying to Obeying

Well, at last we've come to that word, "obey" and I know how unpopular it is in some circles. It's so much easier to just talk about loving the Lord and reading His word and going to church. To talk about obedience is difficult these days, but if we believe that the Bible is the inspired word of God and contains the whole truth of God's message to us, we absolutely cannot ignore this word. Right at the beginning of this chapter, I'm going to give you some scriptures that call us to obedience so that we can understand the importance of not delaying in this part of our love relationship with our Savior.

We must obey God rather than men.

(Acts 5:29)

By faith Abraham, when he was called, obeyed by going out to a place which he was to receive for an inheritance; and he went out not knowing where he was going.

(Hebrews 11:8)

Although He was a Son, He learned obedience from the things which he suffered. And having been made perfect, He became to all those who obey Him the source of eternal salvation.

(Hebrews 5:8-9)

According to the foreknowledge of God the Father, by the sanctifying work of the Spirit, that you may obey Jesus Christ and be sprinkled with His blood: May grace and peace be yours in the fullest measure.

(1 Peter 1:2)

Do you not know that when you present yourselves to someone as slaves for obedience, you are slaves of the one whom you obey, either of sin resulting in death, or of obedience resulting in righteousness? But thanks be to God that though you were slaves of sin, you became obedient from the heart to that form of teaching to which you were committed, and having been freed from sin, you became slaves of righteousness.

(Romans 6:16-18)

....your faith and hope are in God. Since you have in obedience to the truth purified your souls for a sincere love of the brethren, fervently love one another from the heart.

(1 Peter 1:22)

102

To this end also I wrote that I might put you to the test, whether you are obedient in all things.
(2 Corinthians 2:9)

There are many more I could share but I wanted to make sure that we see how important obedience is as we seek to live by faith rather than by feelings. You see, I don't always "feel" like doing the right thing. Sometimes, it feels good to be angry or bitter for a little while. Other times, it feels good to demand my rights or stand up for my selfish motives. But, that is not Godly behavior and it's not living by faith, it's living by what I feel at the moment and then acting upon those feelings. Remember that Godliness is consistent conduct that is consistent with the character of God. To truly live by faith, is to take those unguarded, human feelings and turn them into selfless obedience because of my love for my Lord and my commitment to Him.

2 Corinthians 10:3-5 reminds us,

For though we walk in the flesh, we do not war according to the flesh, for the weapons of our warfare are not of the flesh, but divinely powerful for the destruction of fortresses. We are destroying speculations and every lofty thing raised up against the knowledge of God, and we are taking every thought captive to the obedience of Christ.

To me this means that by the Holy Spirit's power within me, I can take those self-centered feelings and capture the wrong reaction before I act on it. This is my act of loving obedience and God will then honor that act and help me react in a way that honors Him and shows my faith in Him. Remember that faith is "taking God at His word and acting accordingly" and faith is always based on what God says.

103

Let's look at Paul's life for encouragement in this area. Paul had every reason to feel humiliated, forgotten, betrayed, unfairly treated, persecuted and victimized. Let's hear Paul's own description of his life.

Are they servants of Christ? I more so; in far more labors, in far more imprisonments, beaten times without number, often in danger of death. Five times I received from the Jews thirty-nine lashes. Three times I was beaten with rods, once I was stoned three times I was shipwrecked, a night and a day I have spent in the deep. I have been on frequent journeys, in dangers from rivers, dangers from robbers, dangers from my countrymen, dangers from the Gentiles, dangers in the city, dangers in the wilderness, dangers on the sea, dangers among false brethren; I have been in labor and hardship, through many sleepless nights, in hunger and thirst, often without food, in cold and exposure. Apart from such external things, there is the daily pressure upon me of concern for all the churches.

(2 Corinthians 11:23-28)

And yet, just a few verses later he writes that the Lord said to him, *"My grace is sufficient for you, for power is perfected in weakness."* And so Paul responds with captured, obedient thoughts.

...Most gladly, therefore, I will rather boast about my weaknesses, that the power of Christ may dwell in me.

(2 Corinthians 12:9)

I see three important things about Paul's faith.

■ Paul chose to accept whatever God allowed in his life and then he used it for God's glory.

■ Paul's purpose was always to "reflect" or glorify Christ.

■ Paul was always aware of God's power within.

In order to have unlimited, God-honoring faith like Paul, let's look at each one of these carefully. First of all, Paul chose to accept whatever God allowed in his life and then he watched God use it for His glory.

> *Now I want you to know brethren, that my circumstances have turned out for the greater progress of the gospel, so that my imprisonment in the cause of Christ has become well known throughout the whole praetorian guard and to everyone else, and that most of the brethren, trusting in the Lord because of my imprisonment, have far more courage to speak the word of God without fear.*
>
> (Philippians 1:12-14)

Paul is not complaining about his imprisonment or even questioning it. It couldn't have been fun or comfortable or convenient for him, but he chose to see it from God's perspective and recognize that God was using his circumstances for the spread of the gospel. He also realized that the way he handled his imprisonment brought courage to his fellow Christians just as the following story has brought courage to my heart.

"What is it?" Soviet captain Marco snarled at the young boy. "What do you want?" The boy, only twelve, swallowed his fear as he stood before the Communist officer. "Captain, you are the man who

105

put my parents in prison. Today is my mother's birthday, and I always buy her a flower for her birthday. Since my mother taught me to love my enemies and to reward evil with good, I have brought the flower instead for the mother of your children. Please take it home to your wife tonight, and tell her about my love and the love of Christ."

Captain Marco, who had watched unmoved as Christians had been unmercifully beaten and tortured, was stunned at the act of love of this boy. His tears fell as he slowly walked around the desk and grabbed the boy in a fatherly embrace. Marco's heart was changed by the gift of Christ's love. He could no longer arrest and torture Christians, and soon he himself was arrested. Only months after the boy's visit to his office, Marco slumped in a filthy prison cell surrounded by some of the same Christians he had previously arrested and tortured. He tearfully told his cellmates of the young boy and the simple gift of a flower. He considered it an honor to share a cell with those he had previously hunted and attacked.
(from *Extreme Devotion*, Voice of the Martyrs)

What a gift from a child's heart of love and obedience! It changed a man forever! What gift might you give that God could use to change a life?

The gift of humility

The gift of forgiveness

The gift of time

The gift of encouraging words

The gift of sharing the gospel

The gift of giving grace when needed

The gift of understanding

The second thing I recognized about Paul's life was that his only purpose was to glorify Christ. His desire was:

...that with all boldness, Christ shall even now, as always, be exalted in my body whether by life or by death. For to me, to live is Christ...
(Philippians 1:20-21)

For you have been bought with a price, therefore glorify God in your body.
(1 Corinthians 6:20)

So what does it mean to glorify or exalt Christ in my body? I believe that it means that I will allow God, the Holy Spirit, to control my thoughts, my actions and my reactions, no matter what circumstances come my way. Even when I don't understand what God is doing or allowing, I "capture my thoughts" and allow the Holy Spirit to guide me into right thinking and speaking. Even when life seems terribly unfair and I'm deeply hurt, I allow the Holy Spirit to comfort me and lead me to God's truths for discernment and knowledge. Even when friends and family see no point in it, I allow God's Word to penetrate my heart and I act in obedience to it. Even when I come in contact with the unlovely in this world, I welcome the Holy Spirit to reach out in love to that person, through my words and my actions.

A large gang of wild-looking youths began hanging around the little coffee shop where I had been getting my bargain lattes. Each time I'd go, I'd notice them sitting out front and inside, filling the air with their pungent smoke, their fowl language and intimidating all who entered. The owners had tried to get rid of them but to no avail. They were always dressed in black with broken crosses tattooed on their arms. I kept going back because the latte I loved was half as much at this location and I really enjoyed it. However, I didn't like walking through that maze of darkness each time, and I was becoming more perturbed that they had taken over. One night, while thinking about this and telling my husband about it, I was suddenly convicted about my attitude toward them. I asked myself, "Would Jesus walk right through them and ignore them?" and of course, I had to answer that He wouldn't. Now, I know I'm not Jesus, but I do have His power and His Spirit living within me, and I am called to be His ambassador, so I prayed and asked God to help me talk to those young people the next time I went there. I asked that He would help me know what to do and give me the words to say that would somehow show God's love to them. I also thought I'd take a batch of homemade cookies to see if that might help. I was excited to see what God would do.

I went back three days later, ready to see those young people through Jesus' eyes, and to my dismay, the little coffee shop was closed down, for good, and the young people had moved on. I sat in the car and told God how sorry I was that I had delayed speaking to them and showing them that He loved them. I had truly missed an opportunity because of my selfish thoughts. I've been reminded of this many times since and it has helped me choose to obey rather than delay.

The third lesson I see from Paul's life was that he was always aware that everything was done in God's strength alone.

For it is God who is at work in you both to will and to work for His good pleasure.

I can do all things through Him who strengthens me.

He who began a good work in you will perfect it until the day of Jesus Christ.
(Philippians 2:13, 4:13, & 1:6)

So, what does this power mean in our daily lives?

We can trust that God will be with us in every trial and see us through.
Deuteronomy 31:6, Hebrews 13:5

We can trust that God is powerful enough to change anything or any one.
John 16:33, Luke 18:27

We can trust that God will work all things out for our good.
Romans 8:28, Genesis 50:20

We can trust that God is still in control.
Psalm 33:8-11, Proverbs 16:9, Ephesians 1:11

We can trust that God will always love us and nothing can separate us from that love.
Romans 8:35-39

We can trust that God's divine power has granted us everything we need to live godly lives.
2 Peter 1:3

All of these truths should affect how I live as I realize that God's power within me helps me believe and trust Him in all my times. When my children were young and I told them to stop their playing and come in to eat, obedience meant that they were to stop right away and come in. To delay obedience was really disobedience. I've found that when I disobey God in this way, there are always conse- quences such as missed opportunities for growth, a bitter spirit, a broken relationship or a very heavy heart. (James 1:23-25)

Have you delayed obedience in some area of your life? Why not ask for God's forgiveness right now and let Him lift that burden from you.

LORD, GUARD MY HEART

Dear Lord, please guard my lips today
And may they speak for You
Please help me show your love and grace
In all I say and do

Dear Lord, please guard my hands today
May they be used in love
To fix a meal or mend a hurt
Or give a gentle hug

Dear Lord, please guard my thoughts today
And may they honor You
Please help me focus on your truths
So wrong steps will be few.

Dear Lord, please guard my heart today
So I will always be
A servant who delights to say
"Lord, do your work through me."

Carol Hopson

PERSONAL CHECKUP:

If delaying obedience or being disobedient:

You'll always find excuses for your actions or your choice to put off obedience.

Your life will become very self-centered.

You'll think your purpose is to feel good and do what you think is right.

You'll ignore the truths of God's Word that convict you.

Your lack of peace and joy will reveal your lack of faith and love for the Lord.

If desiring to obey:

You'll eagerly search God's Word for guidance in your life.

You'll ask others to hold you accountable.

You'll continually seek to focus on the power and presence of God in your life.

You'll desire to take every thought captive before you act or react.

You'll trust that God is working all things for your good.

Bible Study Questions for Chapter 10 are on page 155.

111

CHAPTER 11

From Prison to Praise

Right now, my ninety-two year old father is lovingly caring for my ninety-one year old mother who has had a major stroke. I told you about her in an earlier chapter and now I want to tell you about my father. He served the Lord for over fifty years as a pastor of several large churches with a radio broadcast for years and a very successful counseling ministry. There was a lot of recognition at times, and he was greatly respected by his peers. I was just visiting my parents three days ago and I was again overwhelmed by what I saw. My parents have been married for over sixty-seven years and have loved each other more each year. Though my mother has made a remarkable recovery since her stroke, there is little she can do and my father takes care of her day and night, including cooking for her, dressing her and taking care of her personal needs. He loves doing it! He loves her! He thanks God every day that God has given him another day to love her and care for her. I must have heard him tell her ten times a day, how much he loves caring for her. And every morning, I heard my father pray for God to give him the strength to take care of his dear bride because he knows he can't do it in his own strength. In this season of his life, he receives no recognition, few thank yous, but just continues to serve the one he loves. It's truly amazing to see this kind of sacrificial love. However, the following story from Chuck Colson's Book entitled *Life Sentence*, tells of the most sacrificial love of all.

> As one who has served time in prison and has since spent most of my life working in them, I'll never forget the most unusual prison I've ever visited. Called Humaita Prison, it is in Sao Jose dos Campos in Brazil. Formerly a government prison, it is now operated by Prison Fellowship Brazil as an alternative prison, without armed guards or high-tech security. Instead, it is run on the Christian principles of love of God and respect for men.
>
> Humaita has only two full-time staff; the rest of the work is done by the 730 inmates serving time for everything from murder and assault to robbery and drug-related crimes. Every man is assigned another inmate to whom he is accountable. In addition, each prisoner is assigned a volunteer mentor from the outside who works with him during his term

and after his release. Prisoners take classes on character development and are encouraged to participate in educational and religious programs.

When I visited this prison, I found the inmates smiling...particularly the murderer who held the keys, opened the gates and let me in. Wherever I walked, I saw men at peace. I saw clean living areas. I saw people working industriously. The walls were decorated with motivational sayings and Scripture. Humaita has an astonishing record. Its recidivism rate is 4 percent, compared to 75 percent in the rest of Brazil. How is that possible?

I saw the answer when my inmate guide escorted me to the notorious cell once used for solitary punishment. Today, he told me, it always houses the same inmate. As we reached the end of the long concrete corridor and he put the key into the lock, he paused and asked, "Are you sure you want to go in?"

"Of course," I replied impatiently. "I've been in isolation cells all over the world." Slowly he swung open the massive door, and I saw the prisoner in that cell: a crucifix, beautifully carved...Jesus, hanging on the cross. "He's doing the time for the rest of us." My guide said softly.

Why should we want to put our faith in Jesus Christ? Because He did the time for you and for me! He paid the price with His life so that we could be free from the "prison" of living by feelings and emotions. One of my treasured memories comes from a retreat where a group of prostitutes, had been invited. A dear elderly woman had been going to the slums to witness to them for years

and she had offered them a weekend away in the mountains, with great food and lots of fun. I don't know how
they got free but six of them decided to come with her. I
was told about them when I arrived at the camp and
they were definitely easy to recognize. I tried to befriend
them right away but they were not about to be drawn in,
especially by the speaker, and so I just continued to try
to sit by them at meals, smile at them whenever I saw
them and let God's love do its work. (They actually tried
to avoid me like the plague!)

The first two meetings were interesting. They sat in
the very back row of a large auditorium and talked,
laughed, chewed gum and were generally distracting.
How I was praying inwardly for them to hear God's love
and somehow respond to it. By Saturday night they
actually seemed to pay more attention or else they were
asleep. Now, we had reached the final meeting on Sunday morning where I usually gave an invitation to accept
Christ as Lord of your life. The first thing I noticed as
we began this final meeting was that all six of those
ladies were sitting on the front row! Were they there to
cause more trouble or were they there to listen...only
God knew.

I concluded with this story that I once heard and never
forgot. A young family was visiting Disneyland and took
their children to see Sleeping Beauty's castle. While inside,
they saw a large group of children surrounding the beautiful, flawless, perfectly adorned Sleeping Beauty. Each child
wanted her attention and the family watched her pose for
numerous photos with her cute, adoring fans. The dad in
the family suddenly noticed an older boy standing in the

corner of the room with his young brother partially hidden behind him. The young boy had a very disfiguring disease and was not like the other children, He couldn't join in with all of the "beautiful children" because he was imperfect, ugly, and difficult to look at. The father who was relating this story remarked that he wished that Sleeping Beauty would notice the small boy and go over to him. But, she was busy touching, posing with and hugging all those around her.

Then suddenly, to his amazement, she noticed the two boys in the corner and she gradually parted the crowd around her and made her way to the frightened, deformed boy. She then squatted down until she was eye level with the little boy and she looked into his sad eyes and smiled. Then, as the crowd watched, she took his deformed face in her hands and she kissed his cheeks, first one side and then the other. "What an incredible moment it was!" the father shared.

It is a story that moved me greatly, but the sad thing was that when she left the little boy, she took her beauty and perfection with her and he was left with his ugly disease. The kiss had only brought momentary joy. As I passed this story on to the women, I shared that when Jesus died on the cross for each of us, He not only kissed us, He took all of our ugliness on Himself and replaced it with His beauty and perfection.

...for He has clothed me with garments of salvation, He has wrapped me with a robe of righteousness...

(Isaiah 61:10)

117

As I closed the service, I asked that anyone who wanted to be clothed in God's pure robe of righteousness and be a new creature in Christ, stay behind and I would come and pray with them. I kept my eyes closed as the women filed out quietly and I prayed for the Holy Spirit to do His work. When I looked up, three of those in the front row remained and were weeping. As I went to them to ask why they had stayed behind, one of them said, "It was that last story! I never knew anyone could make me clean and pure again! Could you help me get that new robe?" What a joy! Before the evening was over, those three who stayed behind had been cleansed, freed from their prison and given eternal life.

JESUS LOVES ME

Jesus loves me this I know
For the Bible tells me so
Then why don't I feel loved sometimes?
Just what goes on inside my mind?

I see those women on TV
And know they don't resemble me
So why should I feel good about
The way my face and frame turned out?

And when I go into a store
And see those tags that say "size 4"
It sets my heart to feeling low
And deals me yet another blow

But Jesus loves me this I know
For the Bible tells me so

So what about me does He love?
How do I look to Him about?

He sees me beautiful in white
Because His Son has paid the price
He sees me pure because He knows
I've given Him my heart and soul.

He sees true beauty in my face
For His love has my fears erased.
He sees me precious and adored
Because I've chosen Him as Lord.

This beauty can't be bought or sold
And best of all it won't grow old
But I must realize the source
And that's my Savior's love, of course!

Yes, Jesus loves me this I know
For His sacrifice did show
He thinks I'm worthy as can be
Oh joy of joys, my God loves me!

Carol Hopson

Are you in some sort of prison? Are the mountains and valleys of your emotions holding you hostage? Jesus loves you and is waiting to break down the bars but *"without faith it is impossible to please God..."* Hebrews 11:6 Why not accept His incredible love and forgiveness and walk on in freedom. To move from feelings to faith is to let God truly be God in your life.

EPILOGUE

A small western town was suffering a severe draught and the people were in danger of losing all their crops, their homes and their future. The town preacher decided to call a prayer meeting in the small church and invite everyone to come and pray for rain. The men and women came dragging in with long faces, and slowly slumped into the rough-hewn pews. A cloud of heaviness and hopelessness seemed to hang over the entire room. Then, just before the preacher began his remarks, a small, smiling, ten-year-old girl came marching down the aisle and sat in the front row. All eyes turned as she strode by because...she was carrying an umbrella!

But , My righteous one shall live by faith, and if he shrinks back, my soul has no pleasure in him.
(Hebrews 10:38)

Are you carrying an umbrella today dear friend?

Dear Heavenly Father,

Thank You, with all my heart, for paying the penalty for my sins, my ugliness, my self-centered thinking and living. Thank You for the new life You've given to each of us who have knelt before You and given our lives to You. Thank You for the great privilege of being Your servant and ambassador here on earth. There's no greater joy than knowing, loving and serving You. Father, forgive me for all the times I've lived by my emotions and feelings instead of living by faith alone. Please help me be a child who trusts You completely and brings joy to You because I'm walking by faith and not by sight. I love You dear Savior!

Your humble servant,
Carol

BIBLE STUDY QUESTIONS

Chapter 1

From Problems to Promises

1. What one problem is foremost in your thoughts today?

2. Do you think you're living by faith or by feelings in regard to your problems, and explain how it is affecting you?

3. In the chart below, list the thoughts your mind has been a magnet for in regard to your problem or problems.

Positive thoughts	Negative thoughts

4. Read the following verses and write out how they would change your thinking in regard to the problem mentioned in question number 1.

Proverbs 3:5-6

Proverbs 3:26

Romans 8:28

Ephesians 4:1-3

Ephesians 4:26-27

Ephesians 5:1-3

2 Corinthians 4:16-18

Galatians 6:9

2 Corinthians 10:4-5

5. Under the Personal Check-up chart, name two things under "living in light of God's promises" that you will ask God to help you put into practice right now.

a.

b.

Chapter 2

From Grit to Grace

1. In what specific area do you need God's enabling grace right now? (In other words, what can't you handle without Him?)

2. Re-read the L I F E choices on page 18 and then make them personal below.

L   What do you need to let go of in obedience to God?

I   Who might God want you to influence for His glory today?

F   Who do you need to forgive today? How will you follow through on this?

E   What will help you begin to express praise continually and are you willing to be obedient in that area?

2. Read Psalm 62 and write down all of the things you can praise God for in any situation.

3. Read Hebrews 13:15 again and write out the four main commands so that they are cemented in your heart.

a.

b.

c.

d.

4. Since we are told to "offer a sacrifice of thanksgiving" in God's Word, what do you need to sacrifice in order to come under submission to God?

Chapter 3

From Regretting to Rejoicing

1. Can you identify a "prison" in your life? (Something that keeps you from freely serving the Lord or living with a peaceful heart)

2. Why do you think you are staying there?

3. Read Philippians 4:6-7 and write out the prerequisites to God's peace.

4. In which of these areas has God shown you that you are being disobedient?

5. Read Psalm 37:1-11 and list all the commands to us as believers and then list what God promises to us.

Commands:

Promises: (also see verses 17, 23-24, 31, 33, 39-40)

Chapter 4

From Selfishness to Godliness

1. Do your thoughts, emotions and goals exhibit a life that seeks happiness or holiness? (be honest)

2. How are you trying to teach or model holiness to those around you? If you find that you're not doing this now, how can you change that?

3. Read I Peter 1:13-16 and write out what you think those "former lusts" are in your life. (See Galatians 5:19-21 and Colossians 3:5-9 for help)

4. After reading Colossians 3:5-17, list below the "clothing" or qualities that we are to throw off and then what we, as believers, are to "put on" or wear.

What should we put off?	What should we put on?

5. Reflect back over the past week and think of how many times you've "opened the door" to fear, doubt, worry, discouragement, etc. and write out how or why you've made that choice.

Read the following verses and tell how you can make the right choice next time you're tempted to "turn around".

Psalm 32:8

Isaiah 26:3

Isaiah 41:10 &13

Galatians 6:9

Jeremiah 32:17

Chapter 5

From Surviving to Thriving

1. In what area of your life do you feel like you're just surviving? Explain.

2. Read 2 Peter 1:3-8 and Colossians 1:9-12 and write out how your thinking should change in response to God's Word.

3. Remember that we are to "throw off the weights" that keep us from running with endurance. What weights do you need to throw off now?

4. How are the weights you listed above affecting your relationships?

With your family:

With your friends or co-workers:

With your Lord:

5. Under the section of "a Marathon requires Patience," which statement do you need to claim and believe today? Write out the statement and the verse that goes with it.

Chapter 6

From Alarmed to Assured

1. Think of the most recent time that you were alarmed (frustrated, fearful) by some news or circumstance you faced. Write out the situation and how you felt.

2. Read James 1:2-4 in this chapter again, from the Message. List the four commands or statements and then write out how you can apply each of these to your situation.

Statement	How I will apply it to my life
a.	
b.	

Statement	How I will apply it to my life

c.

d.

3. How will the following verses assure you of God's love and presence in your life?

Philippians 4:19

Psalm 40:1-3

Jeremiah 31:3

Jeremiah 17:7&8

Psalm 103:17

Philippians 1:6

4. How will you change your daily routine or thought process to be more aware of your "Shepherd's presence" as you go about your day?
   (See Psalm 119:11, 15-16, 27, 33, 37-38 for help)

Chapter 7

From Stumbling Blocks to Stepping Stones

1. List 2 or 3 things in your life that you thought were stumbling blocks and tell how they affected your life.

2. Looking back, can you see how God might have been chiseling away something that didn't resemble Him? Write down what God shows you.

3. Look at the following verses and write out what might need to be "chiseled" from your life.

a. Proverbs 16:18

b. Proverbs 17:14

c. Proverbs 16:2,3

d. Proverbs 15:1

e. Proverbs 20:22

f. Proverbs 22:17

g. Proverbs 21:23

h. Proverbs 28:13

i. Proverbs 28:26

4. Under the Personal Check-up section, choose one way you've seen things as stumbling blocks in your life, and write it out and confess it to the Lord. Then write out one of the ways you want to see your situations in life as stepping stones. (see the list)

Chapter 8

From Feeling to Kneeling

1. Read the opening statements in this chapter again and write out which one most reflects your thoughts today.

2. Sheep needed to be anointed with oil for three reasons. Which type of "anointing" do you need from the Shepherd? (to keep you from irritations, to keep you from conflict, to heal your wounds)

3. How will the following verses help you?

Hebrews 12:14-15

Hebrews 13:5-6

James 1:12

James 1:19-20

James 4:10

James 4:17

4. Read again what the sheep must do to be "anointed" by the shepherd and list them below.

a.

b.

c.

Which one is the most difficult for you to submit to and why?

5. Read Psalm 23 as if you've never read it before. Write five things about the Good Shepherd that stand out to you.

6. Which one of the above will you focus on today and why?

Chapter 9

From Stressed to Blessed

1. When was the last time you felt that the situation you were in wasn't fair to you?

Were you thinking of yourself of the Savior?

2. Read Ephesians 5:15 and 16 and write out how you could have made the most of the opportunity for God's glory.

3. Read Colossians 1:10 and write the four purposes for our lives.

a.

b.

c.

d.

4. How could you have changed your circumstances by being obedient in one or two of these areas?

5. Read Psalm 34:1-4 and then write it out in your own words, making it personal to your life or situation.

6. Read Psalm 46:10 and tell what you think it means to "cease striving" and "know" Who God is?

Chapter 10

From Delaying to Obeying

1. Can you think of something that God wanted you to do but you have delayed obedience (disobeyed) in that area? (forgiving, witnessing, stepping out in faith, submitting, accepting a change in plans, having a forbearing spirit etc.)

2. How important do you think obedience is to the Lord? What does our obedience or disobedience say about our love for Him?

3. Think of something that continually comes up in your life and causes you stress, frustration or worry. Read 2 Corinthians 10:3-5 again and write out three ways you will take your thoughts captive next time, in obedience to the Lord.

a.

b.

c.

4. Look up each verse on the last page of this lesson about trusting God in all situations. Write out a short personal phrase about why or how you will trust God.

Hebrews 13:5 & Deuteronomy 31:6

John 16:33 & Luke 18:27

Romans 8:28 & Genesis 50:20

Psalms 33:8-11, Proverbs 16:9 & Ephesians. 1:11

Romans 8:35-39

2 Peter 1:3

5. Write out a prayer of commitment to the Lord, asking for help in the area of quickly obeying His Word and His leading in your life.

Chapter 11

From Prison and Praise

1. In what area of your life do you need to ask God for strength every day?

2. How do you see this daily prayer making a difference in your life? See Isaiah 40:28-31 for your answers.

3. When Jesus died on the cross, He took all our ugliness on Himself and replaced it with His righteousness. How should His righteousness look in our lives?

Hebrews 10:38

John 14:15, 23-24

John 15:5

John 15:12

Galatians 2:20

Colossians 3:1-2

Colossians 4:2, 5-6

4. As you complete this book and Bible study, write out the area(s) in which God has convicted you the most.

5. Now write out the area in which you have been most encouraged to live by faith and not feelings, and then pray and ask God to help you be faithful to that new commitment.